Tana's
kitchen secrets

Tana's
kitchen secrets

MITCHELL BEAZLEY

Contents

Introduction

I want this book to help you to love cooking. I've written it for people who enjoy food but who, like me, suddenly find they needed to expand their recipe repertoire and their cooking skills – either because they have a family to feed or for some other reason. I now cook a variety of dishes every day. My four kids always have a homemade meal after school, and then I make something for Gordon and me later in the evening. And I love to plan weekends filled with nurturing, delicious food that we can all share.

I cook because I want to be confident about what my family eats. I want to feel sure that the meat is good, or that the bread is wholesome and nutritious. Our kids know what fresh food tastes like and I am glad this is the norm for them, not something they'll have to learn. I want your children to be the same.

With a busy life, I don't have hours to spend shopping, prepping and planning dinner. Quite often, food is bought on the way home and meals are made in the minimum of time…but I want maximum results. These recipes will help you to achieve that, too.

Don't be scared to teach yourself to cook – I did! Use my recipes as a guideline: if you can't find an ingredient, don't panic. When I was making my Haddock & Spring Vegetable Risotto (*see* page 112), I didn't have the parsley I was going to use, so I added mint…and it was much better! Always add your favourite ingredients and leave out anything you're not so keen on. The only rule is to taste all the time, so you'll know when you're on the right road.

Remember that your family needs a balanced diet. I always try to remind myself to eat as much fish as I do meat and sometimes (much to Gordon's horror) sneak in a vegetarian day!

We have a good butcher and fishmonger but, if you're not so lucky, don't worry. I also buy meat from a supermarket that employs a proper butcher. Always talk to the person behind the counter when you've found someone you trust. They can tell you what cut of meat to choose and how to cook it, or what fish to put in a pie (*see* pages 88–9), when it needs to taste great but it doesn't matter what it looks like. Let them advise you, because they know what they are doing. And they can save you money, too.

Every family needs time around the table. The best times are when all six of us are together. When you sit down as a family, you hear about who got a star for their maths, or who got into the lacrosse team. We've got to stay close to our kids so they can tell us these things, and around the table is the perfect place. This book will help you make those wonderful family meals, so enjoy it!

Kitchen kit secrets

Here are some of what I consider to be the essential pieces of equipment that you should have in your kitchen.

Pans Every cook needs a good selection of pans with lids. They must be dishwasher-proof and nonstick – especially for scrambled egg, unless you love washing up! It's handy to have an ovenproof pan, so you can transfer a piece of meat or fish directly from the hob to the oven.

Knives and sharpeners The sharper the knives, the less likely you are to cut yourself, however weird that may sound. So you must have a knife sharpener.

Microplane grater Fantastic for grating everything from citrus zest to Parmesan. My favourite broke recently after a very long life and I was mortified.

Cheese shaver To make neat slices for sandwiches.

Food processor For easy curry pastes. To save time, I also use it to chop onions. It makes sauces so much easier and less time-consuming.

Sieves Have a tiny sieve – or even a tea strainer – for dusting the top of cakes and tarts (*see* page 138), for instant prettification.

Scissors You'll need a good strong pair of these, hidden so they can't be stolen by the kids and end up getting covered in glitter and glue!

Mixing bowls I love Pyrex. Gordon likes metal bowls, but they always remind me of dog bowls. So he has his cupboard with his bowls and I have mine with my Pyrex.

Plastic spatulas I have three spatulas – small, medium and large – and I am obsessive about them.

Cake tins I love loaf tins for banana loaves or Cherry & Almond Loaf (*see* page 248), which I make frequently. I also have a couple of round cake tins, and muffin and cupcake tins.

Cookie cutters I'm a bit like a child in a toy shop when I see these – you can never have too many shapes!

Digital kitchen scales Essential.

Oven gloves Don't use dish cloths to move hot dishes and baking sheets as it's far easier to burn yourself. Use gloves, preferably a pair that cover your skin up to the elbows.

Dish cloths Always place a dish cloth under your chopping board so it doesn't slip. This will save your fingers from many nicks.

Small chopping board These are great for those times when you want to chop only a small amount of something. Mine is used regularly for the lemons and limes for our evening gin and tonic.

Large chopping board I use wooden chopping boards as platters for cold meats and cheese: they look so attractive.

Olive oil The very best thing for wooden surfaces around your kitchen sink, and for chopping boards. It's protective and prevents mould and warping.

Storecupboard secrets

Below are some tips on what food items you should have in your storecupboard at all times so that you are always prepared to whip up a quick, tasty meal.

Stock up your larder Don't feel daunted by the length of this list: you can collect things a little at a time. Make sure you have some chutneys, tomato purée, canned tomatoes, coconut milk and sweetcorn. I keep Worcestershire sauce, ketchup, brown sauce and grain mustard. Make sure you have baking powder, self-raising and plain flours and caster and granulated sugars for baking, as well as dried yeast and vanilla essence (pods if you're feeling flush). You'll need basmati, risotto and red rices, couscous, lentils and dried pasta shapes with a jar of pesto. I wouldn't be without miso paste, and it's handy to have Thai red curry paste for prawns (*see* page 92) and Thai green curry paste for chicken. Hoisin and soy sauces, white and red wine vinegars will lift the flavour of many sauces. Lastly, have a jar of blossom honey.

Refrigerator Start your weekend with a full refrigerator. We have salad, cheese (always a nice block of Parmesan), ham and chorizo, marinated artichokes, anchovies and peppers, fresh pasta, low-fat crème fraîche, pancetta, vine tomatoes, free-range eggs and fresh vegetables. And a beautiful chicken. So there's always something to eat, even if it's just scrambled eggs.

Get ahead Try to have biscuit doughs in the refrigerator, rolled into sausage shapes and wrapped in clingfilm so you can instantly bake – the house will smell delicious. That aroma has the same effect on me as piles of clean, fluffy laundry – it's so comforting!

The vegetable rack Have chillies, garlic and onions, ready for all sorts of sauces.

Freezer I always have Frozen Fruit (*see* page 221), frozen peas and sweetcorn. If I have a busy week ahead, I'll freeze a pot of Chicken Cacciatore (*see* page 34) to have an emergency meal in hand.

Baked beans Vital for an instant supper for Gordon and me. We'll have toast spread with Marmite, the beans, then cheese and Worcestershire sauce on top. If you're feeling extravagant, crown the whole stack with a fried egg!

Spices Keep spices in a dark cupboard to preserve their flavour. I use both white and black peppercorns, chilli powder and garam masala, ground cumin, coriander and cinnamon, star anise, cinnamon sticks and cloves. Buy kaffir lime leaves and curry leaves in bulk from Asian shops – they freeze wonderfully.

Hot sauce We get through a lot of this and it all goes into our son Jack! There's always someone who wants to put hot sauce on everything, so it's good to have a bottle handy.

Oil You'll need mild vegetable and olive oils for everyday cooking, and a bottle of good stuff for drizzling over salads and fish. Never cook with expensive olive oil, as the precious aromas are destroyed by heat.

Sprinkles I collect these, and have some great multi-coloured dinosaurs at the moment! Like a magpie, you can pick up interesting shapes and colours. There are always school cake sales and it can get competitive with other mums…you need to stay ahead of the game!

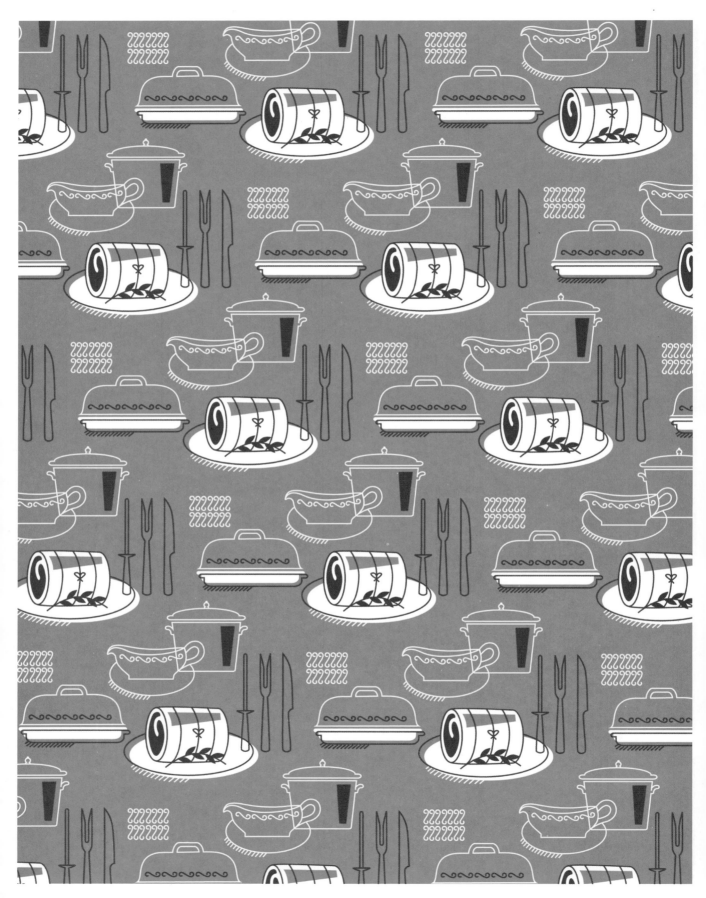

Slow & easy meat

Really rustic shoulder of lamb · Shepherd's pie · Lauren's meatballs
Crackling roast pork · Spicy beef stew · Parmesan chicken drumsticks
Chicken cacciatore · Chicken broth · Poached whole chicken
Roast guinea fowl with lemon & garlic

Secrets of slow & easy meat

When you slow cook, you can choose the cheaper cuts, such as shoulder of lamb or braising steak, that need time in the oven for the sinews to tenderise. And the slower you cook them, the more they relax. Not only does this free you up from the stove while it putters away, but it also fills your home with a delicious aroma. Your family will know that dinner is going to be wonderful.

If you have a young family, these recipes are ideal. Because they are very forgiving and don't need exact timing, you won't have to cook twice, once for the kids and once for yourself. You can put a recipe such as my Chicken Cacciatore (*see* page 34) in the oven while the children are doing their homework. Then they can eat early and you can leave the pot on a very low heat so that, like Gordon and me, the grown-ups can eat it later.

It's easy to turn slow-cooked dishes into other meals, which is excellent news if, as I do, you hate waste. When I make Really Rustic Shoulder of Lamb (*see* page 16), I turn the leftover flaked meat into a curry for the kids, adding vegetables, garam masala, cumin, mango chutney and yogurt.

Every week you should cook a meal with minced meat… I love it! It's so versatile. I start off with a basic bolognese for the children, then Gordon and I spice it up into chilli con carne for our meal, with some judicious seasonings. Minced meat reheats and freezes like a dream. It's my standby dish.

When I was growing up we had a roast every Sunday, though we have it only once or twice a month now. You'll need a day when you have an hour to see to it, so choose a bleak, chilly afternoon. It's important to have decent family time together, and my Crackling Roast Pork (*see* page 27) makes a wonderful, warming, winter family meal.

In this chapter you'll find the best recipe to have up your sleeve when you're faced with sports day and the requisite picnic. My Poached Whole Chicken (*see* page 38) is incredibly easy. It must be served at room temperature, so lends itself brilliantly to picnic hampers. Never serve it chilled; I hate fridge-cold food. Take it to the picnic and eat with lashings of Tomato & Tarragon Mayonnaise (*see* page 272) and New Potato Salad with Crème Fraîche & Coriander (*see* page 188).

Really rustic shoulder of lamb

This is one of the cheapest cuts of lamb available and is suitable for a succulent slow roast as it has lots of hard-working fibres that break down over a long cooking time. The richer-tasting mutton would be excellent for this recipe as well.

Serves 4
Preparation time 5–10 minutes
Cooking time 3 hours 30 minutes

1.8kg (4lb) shoulder of lamb, bone in
1 tsp dried thyme
1 tsp dried marjoram
1 tsp coriander seeds
1 tsp ground cinnamon
salt flakes and black pepper
3 tbsp olive oil
2 rosemary sprigs

1 Preheat the oven to 200°C/400°F/gas mark 6.

2 Pat the lamb dry with kitchen paper (*see* secret, page 27). Using a small, sharp knife, make slits all over the shoulder, each about 2.5cm (1in) long. Grind together all the dried herbs and spices in a mortar and pestle until you have a powder. Season, add the oil and mix to a paste. Rub it all over the lamb shoulder and down into all the slits.

3 Place the lamb and rosemary into a roasting dish and put in the oven for 25–30 minutes, to colour up nicely. Take the lamb out of the oven and cover with foil, sealing tightly around the edges. Turn the oven down to 160°C/325°F/gas mark 3 and return the meat to the oven for 3 hours, until it can be easily flaked with a fork.

4 Remove the lamb from the oven and allow it to rest for 10 minutes, then flake the meat off the bone. Mix it with the juices in the roasting dish. Serve on a platter on the table for everyone to help themselves.

Choosing the right lamb

Look for lamb that has been hung for 1–2 weeks, as it will be good eating, tender and have a full flavour. A butcher will help, and may be able to tell you where the meat came from and which breed it is. Meat from a young lamb will look pink, while the meat of an older animal should be reddish in hue.

Shepherd's pie

Over the years I have made my mum's version of this dish, my mother-in-law's recipe and invented my own too, gradually adding more ingredients and trying to modernise it. However, this is a very traditional pie and less is more in this case. It's great served with peas.

Serves 6–8
Preparation time 20 minutes
Cooking time 40 minutes
Can be made in advance
Suitable for freezing

2 tbsp olive oil
1kg (2lb 4oz) minced lamb
salt flakes and black pepper
2 tbsp tomato purée
1 large onion, finely chopped
1 garlic clove, finely chopped
3 carrots, finely chopped
1 celery stalk, finely chopped
leaves from 2 rosemary sprigs, finely chopped
1½ tbsp gravy granules
2 tbsp brown sauce
good dash of Worcestershire sauce

For the mash
2.25kg (5lb) Maris Piper potatoes
large knob of butter
splash of milk
2 free-range egg yolks

1 Pour half the oil into a frying pan over a medium heat, add the lamb and season. Turn and break up the meat with a wooden spoon and allow it to brown all over; keep stirring or it might burn. Tip it into a colander to drain off the fat.

2 Add the remaining oil to the frying pan over a medium heat and return the lamb to the pan. Add the tomato purée and stir to coat for 1–2 minutes, then mix in the onion, garlic, carrots, celery and rosemary. Season again, stir and allow the vegetables to soften.

3 Mix the gravy granules with 600ml (1 pint) boiling water, then add it to the pan with the brown sauce. Let the liquid simmer gently and reduce slightly, then stir in the Worcestershire sauce. Leave to simmer gently for 20 minutes. Preheat the oven to 200°C/400°F/gas mark 6.

4 Meanwhile, make the mash. Cut the potatoes into even-sized pieces and put them in a saucepan. Add enough cold water to cover and a good pinch of salt, then bring to the boil over a high heat. Reduce the heat and simmer for 15 minutes, or until tender. Drain well (*see* secret, left) and mash with the butter and milk, season, then add the egg yolks (to help the topping colour well) and stir rapidly.

5 Place the lamb into a 2.5-litre (4½-pint) ovenproof dish and cover with the mash. Fork the top gently to ensure a lovely crunchy topping. Cook in the oven for 20 minutes, until bubbling gently and golden brown with lovely crispy bits.

Perfect mash

Your cooked potatoes should be as dry as possible, to avoid horrid watery mash. After draining, return them to the pan over a low heat for a few minutes, watching so they don't scorch, until all the steam has been driven off. Try adding sweet potato, parsnip or celeriac for delicious variations, but always include potato for smoothness. Then, of course, mash in lashings of butter and milk, cream or sour cream.

Lauren's meatballs

Lauren is a totally self-taught cook who has worked for Gordon for a couple of years. I was moaning to her that I wanted to cook more meatballs and she gave me this fabulous recipe. She has an amazing ability to put flavours together in an easy and inspiring way.

Serves 4
Preparation time 20 minutes
Cooking time 40–45 minutes
Can be made in advance to end of step 4

1 tbsp olive oil, plus extra for the baking tray
2.5cm (1in) fresh root ginger, peeled
    and finely chopped
2 garlic cloves, crushed
1 large onion, finely sliced
1 aubergine, cut into 1cm (½in) dice
3 tbsp medium curry paste
400ml can coconut milk
300ml (½ pint) chicken stock
salt flakes and black pepper
juice of ½ lime

For the meatballs
500g (1lb 2oz) minced lamb
large handful of flatleaf parsley leaves,
    roughly chopped
small handful of mint leaves,
    roughly chopped
1 free-range egg yolk
2 tbsp tomato purée

1 To make the sauce, heat the oil in a large non-stick frying pan over a medium heat, add the ginger, garlic and onion and stir for 10 minutes, or until softened and translucent but not coloured. Add the aubergine and continue to cook for 5–10 minutes until soft. Stir in the curry paste, then add the coconut milk and stock. Bring to a simmer, season and cook for 25–30 minutes.

2 For the meatballs, place the minced lamb in a mixing bowl and add the chopped herbs and egg yolk, stir in the tomato purée, season and mix until everything is evenly combined. Roll the mixture into 16 small balls (*see* secret, below left), put them on a plate, cover and place in the refrigerator for 20 minutes to firm up. Preheat the oven to 220°C/425°F/gas mark 7.

3 Place the meatballs on to an oiled baking tray and cook for 10–15 minutes, turning once halfway through, until nicely browned all over.

4 Meanwhile, pour the sauce into a blender and process until smooth. You may have to do this in batches as the blender should be no more than half full each time to avoid an overspill; hold the lid on with a dish cloth to protect your hands from splashes. Pour the puréed sauce into a large saucepan and carefully add the meatballs.

5 Simmer gently for 20 minutes. Taste, adjust the seasoning and stir in the lime juice to lift the flavourings. These are great served on a bed of steamed basmati rice.

Shaping meatballs, burgers and koftas

When shaping minced meat into meatballs, burgers or koftas, always have a bowl of cold water to hand. Wet your hands before shaping and rolling the meat into equal-sized balls. This helps to make the mixture more pliable and stops it sticking to your hands. Always chill the shaped meatballs, burgers or koftas before cooking to firm them up, making them less likely to fall apart.

Crackling roast pork

This is a great traditional Sunday roast and so simple to do. Have it with some roast vegetables; you'll find plenty of recipes in the Vegetables chapter (see pages 152–89). Don't be worried about making excellent crackling; the easy tips here work a treat.

Serves 4
Preparation time 10 minutes
Cooking time 1 hour 20 minutes,
   plus 30 minutes resting

1kg (2lb 4oz) boneless pork leg joint,
   rind scored
1–2 tbsp salt
black pepper
4 tbsp olive oil

1 Preheat the oven to 220°C/425°F/gas mark 7. You need this blast of heat to seal the meat and give the crackling a good head start.

2 Dry the joint (*see* secret, below left). Score the fat diagonally at 2.5cm (1in) intervals, first in one direction, then in the other, to produce a diamond pattern. Rub the salt all over the fat, getting well into the scored slits, season with pepper and drizzle with oil. Cook in a roasting dish for 30 minutes, or until the crackling is blistered and golden.

3 Turn the oven down to 160°C/325°F/gas mark 3 and cook the pork for a further 50 minutes. To check it is cooked through, slide a knife into the centre of the joint, leave for 10 seconds, then remove and touch the tip to the inside of your arm where it is sensitive to heat. If it's really hot, the pork is cooked. The juices should run clear with no trace of pink.

4 Turn off the oven and leave the pork inside to rest for 20 minutes, then remove and rest for 10 minutes more at room temperature. Meanwhile, skim the fat from the juices and put them into a small pan over a high heat to reduce to an intense, thin gravy.

5 Serve the pork with the gravy and my Chunky Apple Sauce (*see* page 280) and accompany with roast carrots and parsnips.

Preparing meat for roasting

With this or any other joint of red meat, a good habit to get into is to let it air-dry before roasting. It will give pork better crackling, while lamb and beef will become crisp at the edges. Pat the meat as dry as possible with kitchen paper, then leave the joint, uncovered, at room temperature for an hour – or overnight in the refrigerator – to allow the remaining moisture to evaporate.

Spicy beef stew

A really quick, one-pot dish that you can leave slow-cooking in the oven. The long cooking time allows the spices to develop a wonderfully rounded flavour. This is also a great storecupboard dish, needing very few fresh ingredients. Serve with lots of fluffy white rice.

Serves 4
Preparation time 10 minutes
Cooking time 1 hour 45 minutes
Can be made in advance
Suitable for freezing

500g (1lb 2oz) braising steak,
   cut into 2.5cm (1in) dice
pinch of salt
2 tsp garam masala
1 tsp chilli powder
1 tbsp plain flour
4 tbsp vegetable oil
4 carrots, cut into 2.5cm (1in) dice
2 tbsp tomato purée
4 star anise
1 cinnamon stick
1 dried chilli, finely chopped
2 × 400g cans chopped tomatoes
2 bay leaves
black pepper

1 Preheat the oven to 180°C/350°F/gas mark 4. Place the steak into a large mixing bowl with a good pinch of salt, the garam masala, chilli powder and flour. Mix so all the beef is coated.

2 Pour 3 tbsp of the oil into a large flameproof casserole over a medium-high heat. When the oil is simmering, add the beef and cook, turning, until all sides have a good colour (*see* secret, below). Place the beef in a colander over a bowl to allow excess fat to drain off.

3 Add the remaining oil to the casserole, add the carrots and allow them to colour slightly, stirring so they do not stick or burn. Return the meat to the casserole and add the tomato purée. Stir for 2–3 minutes so the purée is cooked through. Toss in the star anise, cinnamon, dried chilli, tomatoes, bay leaves, black pepper and 200ml (7fl oz) boiling water. Season well and cover.

4 Transfer the casserole to the oven and cook for 1 hour 30 minutes. Check it every now and then – if the stew seems to be thickening too much, add a little more boiling water. At the end of cooking, turn off the oven, open the door slightly and let the dish cool for 10–20 minutes. The beef should be lovely and tender with a good kick of spice.

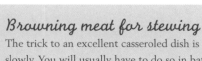

Browning meat for stewing

The trick to an excellent casseroled dish is to brown the meat very well before stewing slowly. You will usually have to do so in batches as, if a pan is overcrowded, the meat will steam and never take on a good caramelised colour. Fry your chosen meat, turning occasionally, until all sides are dark gold, to bring out a wonderfully savoury, roasted taste along with an inherent sweetness.

Parmesan chicken drumsticks

Try this delicious recipe with other cuts of chicken such as goujons or thighs, but remember that the boneless goujons will need far less time in the oven to cook through; start checking them after 10–15 minutes and don't leave them in for too long or they will dry out.

Serves 4
Preparation time 5 minutes
Cooking time 35–40 minutes
Can be made in advance to end of step 3
Suitable for freezing at end of step 3

50g (1¾oz) butter
1 tbsp olive oil, plus extra for the
    baking sheet
16 chicken drumsticks, skin on
225g (8oz) Parmesan cheese, finely grated
2 tbsp dried oregano
2 tbsp paprika
2 tsp dried parsley
salt flakes and black pepper
crisp, green salad, to serve

1 Preheat the oven to 190°C/375°F/gas mark 5.

2 Melt the butter in a saucepan over a low heat, then add the oil. Pour into a mixing bowl, add the chicken, and turn to ensure the drumsticks are evenly coated.

3 Mix together the Parmesan, oregano, paprika and parsley in another bowl and season well. Drop each buttered drumstick into the mixture, turning until all sides are well coated and pressing the meat well to make sure the coating sticks. (Alternatively, *see* secret, below.) At this point you can cover and refrigerate the drumsticks for a few hours until ready to use – this often helps the coating to adhere – but bring them back to room temperature before cooking.

4 Place the drumsticks on a lightly oiled baking sheet. Bake for 35 minutes, until golden and crispy, turning once halfway through cooking. To check they are cooked, insert a small, sharp knife or skewer into the thickest part of the drumstick, piercing right to the bone, then remove. The juices that come out should run clear; if there is any trace of pink, return the drumsticks to the oven for 5 minutes, then test again.

5 Serve with a crisp, green salad.

Applying coatings to meat

To save on washing up, place the coating ingredients in a large resealable food bag and shake to combine. Add the meat, seal the bag and shake it well until the meat is evenly coated. Massage the meat through the bag to press the coating on firmly.

Chicken cacciatore

This recipe is not at all like the classic dish with the same title, but the name has stuck in our home! It is a really quick and easy supper requiring minimum effort. I usually serve it with buttered baked potatoes. You can use 1kg (2lb 4oz) of very ripe fresh tomatoes instead of canned if you prefer.

Serves 4 hungry children, with seconds
Preparation time 15–20 minutes
Cooking time 1 hour 15 minutes
Can be made in advance to end of step 5
Suitable for freezing at end of step 5

2 tbsp olive oil
1 onion, finely chopped
2 garlic cloves, finely chopped
salt flakes and black pepper
2 tbsp finely chopped rosemary leaves
6 canned anchovies, roughly chopped
1 tbsp tomato purée
3 × 400g cans cherry tomatoes
handful of fresh parsley leaves,
    finely chopped
6 free-range chicken legs, skin on

Which cut to choose?
Chicken legs are ideal for this dish. Choose plump pieces with undamaged skin. Legs are cheap and have the dark meat that is best for casseroles and other slow-cooked dishes as it remains moist, whereas chicken breasts will soon dry out. Breasts should be reserved for quicker cooking to keep them juicy and succulent. You could also try making this and other slow-cooked recipes with inexpensive chicken wings, though they will cook more quickly than legs (start checking for doneness after 25 minutes).

1 Preheat the oven to 190°C/375°F/gas mark 5.

2 Pour half the oil into a deep frying pan and place over a medium heat. Add the onion and garlic, adding a pinch of salt, and cook for 10 minutes, or until soft but not coloured. Add the rosemary and anchovies, allowing the anchovies to break up and almost melt into the onions and garlic. Stir in the tomato purée.

3 Add the canned tomatoes (or fresh if you have the patience to skin them!), season well and simmer for 10–15 minutes until the sauce begins to thicken. Stir in half the parsley.

4 Meanwhile, heat the remaining oil in a separate frying pan over a medium heat and brown the chicken legs on all sides. As well as making the chicken crispy, this will render and remove a fair amount of the fat.

5 Remove the chicken legs from the pan with a slotted spoon and place in an ovenproof dish with a close-fitting lid. Pour the tomato sauce over the top and put the lid on. Bake for 40 minutes, or until cooked through. To check it is ready, pierce the thickest part of a chicken leg with a small, sharp knife, right down to the bone, then remove. If the juices that come out run clear, it is ready. If there is even a trace of pink, return to the oven for 5 minutes, then test again.

6 Sprinkle over the remaining parsley before serving.

Chicken broth

I give this to the kids when they come home late from swimming or other sports. Add any vegetables that you want to this deep-flavoured, savoury soup. Crunchy green beans, mangetouts, broccoli florets, sugarsnap peas and baby sweetcorn are particularly nice here. You can also choose to keep the broth plain, without vegetables or cream. Either way, it's restorative and calming.

Serves 4 as a starter
Preparation time 5–10 minutes
Cooking time 2 hours
Can be made in advance
Suitable for freezing

8 free-range chicken drumsticks
1 large onion, cut into wedges
2 carrots, cut into 2.5cm (1in) chunks
1 leek, roughly chopped
2cm (¾in) fresh root ginger, peeled and
    roughly chopped
2 bay leaves
2 kaffir lime leaves
small handful of lemon thyme sprigs
2 stems of lemon grass, bashed
2 tsp coriander seeds
1 tsp white peppercorns
2 star anise
salt flakes and black pepper
200g (7oz) selected vegetables, chopped
    (*see* recipe introduction)
142ml pot double cream (optional)

1 Place the drumsticks into a stock pot or large saucepan. Pour in 2 litres (3½ pints) cold water, or enough to cover. Bring to the boil over a gentle heat, skim off any scum that rises to the surface, then add all the other ingredients except the selected vegetables and the cream. Keep on a really low simmer for about 2 hours, skimming any scum and adding water when necessary to keep the ingredients covered.

2 Add your vegetables and simmer gently until crisp but tender (about 5 minutes, depending on which vegetables you choose) and stir in some cream, if you like. Strain through a large sieve into a bowl, reserving any chicken meat you may want to shred into the broth. Season to taste and serve piping hot.

Making your own stock

Homemade stock is a great way to use up cooked chicken bones and carcasses (the drumsticks here give a richer taste). Naturally, use beef bones instead for beef stock, and so on. Always cover the bones with cold water; as the water comes to the boil, the fat comes to the surface, at which point you can skim it off. Add any flavourings that you like, remembering that onions and carrots give a delicate sweetness. Skim to remove impurities and prevent cloudiness. Use at once, or freeze.

Poached whole chicken

This is a great item to have in the refrigerator for packed lunches, picnics or salads as the chicken stays lovely and moist throughout. If you are using it in a salad, add Jersey Royals, warm asparagus or my Tomato & Tarragon Mayonnaise (see page 272).

Serves 4
Preparation time 5–10 minutes
Cooking time 1 hour 40 minutes
Can be made in advance

1 whole, free-range chicken, about
   1.7kg (3lb 12oz)
1 tbsp coriander seeds
1 tbsp white peppercorns
3 bay leaves
4 rosemary sprigs
1 tbsp salt flakes
4 garlic cloves
1 celery stalk, roughly chopped
1 carrot, halved
1 onion, quartered

1 Place the chicken in a very large pan. Fill with enough cold water just to cover, then add all the other ingredients.

2 Bring to the boil over a medium heat, reduce the heat to the lowest possible temperature, cover and simmer very gently for 1 hour 30 minutes, until you can easily remove a leg from the body. Set aside to cool a little in the stock and skim the top if necessary.

3 Remove the chicken from the pan, peel off and discard the skin and cut into joints. Strain the stock into a bowl; it is brilliant as a soup base and can be frozen for later use if preferred.

Why free range is best for both palate and poultry

Although a free-range chicken is more expensive than a battery bird, it will more than make up for its price in both flavour and the quality of broth its bones produce. As these birds are older than their battery peers, their carcasses are more developed, so the stock they make contains more protein – and savoury deliciousness – while you can feel sure the chickens' lives have been happier, too.

Roast guinea fowl with lemon & garlic

This is a very easy, rustic dish and is delicious served with minted peas. Guinea fowl is a lean meat with a lot of flavour and makes a great alternative to chicken. It's not gamey enough to upset sensitive palates, and it has an interesting taste that makes it a popular dish.

Serves 4
Preparation time 15 minutes
Cooking time 45 minutes

1.3kg (3lb) guinea fowl
olive oil, for the dish,
    plus extra to drizzle if necessary
salt flakes and black pepper
1 garlic bulb, broken into cloves,
    skin left on
4 thyme sprigs
2 rosemary sprigs
1 unwaxed lemon, cut into wedges
2 carrots, roughly chopped
350g (12oz) new potatoes
1 red onion, cut into wedges

1 Preheat the oven to 200°C/400°F/gas mark 6. Joint the guinea fowl (*see* secret, below).

2 Lightly oil a deep ovenproof dish and add the guinea fowl. Sprinkle with seasoning and roll the joints to coat. Add the garlic, herb sprigs and lemon wedges. Cook in the oven for 20–25 minutes.

3 Meanwhile, bring a large pan of water to the boil over a high heat, add the carrots and potatoes and boil for 5–10 minutes, until half cooked. Drain and set aside.

4 Remove the guinea fowl from the oven, add the carrots, potatoes and onion to the dish and drizzle over a little more oil if the bird seems dry. Return to the oven for 10–15 minutes. Check the guinea fowl is cooked by piercing through the thickest part of a thigh to the bone with a skewer; the juices should run clear. Remove the garlic, herb sprigs and lemon wedges before serving.

Jointing poultry

Arm yourself with sturdy kitchen scissors or, even better, poultry shears. Turn the bird on its breast and remove the backbone. Feel where the thighs attach to the body, cut through, then separate the drumsticks from the thighs. Chop either side of the breastbone to remove both breasts and wings, then halve each so that one piece has the wing attached. Snip off the wing tips. Trim all the pieces and reserve the bones and trimmings for stock.

Quick & easy meat

Indian lamb chops · Homemade lamb sausages in prosciutto

Lamb kidneys in cream & mushroom sauce · Pork loin with pancetta & sage

Pork chops with honey & mustard glaze · Simple pork stir-fry

Breaded veal escalopes with mozzarella & tomato & red pepper sauce

Rump steak flavoured with anchovy & garlic · Spicy chicken wings

Marinated duck breasts · Chinese duck breast wraps

Turkey escalopes with mashed butternut squash & corn on the cob

Turkey masala kebabs

Secrets of quick & easy meat

Meats that are quick to cook tend to be more expensive than others. Tender cuts, such as steak and chops, need just a blast of heat to seal and you pay for the fact that the meat isn't sinewy and tough. But with some recipes you can't skimp. The way to make it work for your family budget is to buy the main ingredient – the duck breast or pork loin – first, then plan around it with cheap, seasonal vegetables. I love steak, salad and chips – it's my favourite meal in the world – but it's always a treat. And there's never even a tiny bit wasted.

But many quick-cook meats won't harm your wallet. My Spicy Chicken Wings (*see* page 62) are economical and popular with everyone.

Another inexpensive way to approach quick meat is to use offal. It's easy to feel squeamish about this, but my Lamb Kidneys in Cream & Mushroom Sauce (*see* page 50) are delicious and full of iron and essential nutrients. Previous generations were well aware of the health benefits of eating offal and, though I'm not a massive fan, I do eat it because it's good for me and my family.

Everyone should know how to prepare a stir-fry (*see* page 56). It's a healthy, quick and easy dish that's great for using up leftovers. There are no rules about what you can and can't include. The only thing to remember is not to leave it in the pan for too long: you want fresh, crunchy vegetables.

Kebabs are a wonderful secret weapon to have in your repertoire and you should try my Turkey Masala Kebabs (*see* page 67). Children always love them, especially if they've helped to thread the skewers, and they're fun to eat.

Lamb chops are among the most versatile and speedy of main-course meats and we eat them a lot in our house. They take wonderfully to all sorts of strong seasonings, such as those in my recipe for Indian Lamb Chops (*see* page 46), and they also go well with tomato, rosemary and garlic.

You can't just leave these dishes to cook, as you can some of the recipes in the Slow & Easy Meat chapter (*see* pages 12–41), and they need more monitoring than oven-baked dishes. So I often cook these quicker dishes for Gordon and myself later in the evenings when my hands are free from children.

Indian lamb chops

This wonderfully warming dish is delicious with my Healthy Couscous (see page 118) and with the broccoli and almond accompaniment on page 54. And, of course, it's great to have a lot of recipes for chops in your culinary arsenal!

Serves 2
Preparation time 10 minutes,
 plus 30 minutes–1 hour marinating
Cooking time 20 minutes
Can be made in advance to end of step 1

150ml (5fl oz) natural yogurt
1 garlic clove, crushed
2 tbsp ground coriander
1 tsp ground turmeric
1 tbsp coriander seeds, crushed
1 tsp paprika
juice of 1 lime
20g (¾oz) coriander leaves
salt flakes and black pepper
4 lamb loin chops
Healthy Couscous, My Style
 (*see* page 118), to serve

1 Place all the ingredients except the lamb into a large bowl and mix well together. Add the lamb chops and toss them in this marinade, to coat well. Cover the bowl with clingfilm and set aside to marinate in the refrigerator for between 30 minutes and 1 hour.

2 Preheat the oven to 200°C/400°F/gas mark 6.

3 Remove the chops from the marinade and place them into an ovenproof dish (discard the marinade). Cook in the oven for about 20 minutes for meat that is a little pink in the centre – perfect for me – or leave them for 5–10 minutes longer if you prefer well-done meat.

4 Serve hot accompanied by my Healthy Couscous.

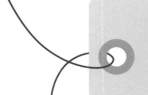

Why use a yogurt marinade?

Yogurt is an invaluable secret weapon in a meat marinade, as the peoples of the Far East and subcontinent have always known. Its cultures and mild acidity mean it penetrates right through the meat and acts as a tenderiser, breaking down the tough fibres to prepare the pieces for cooking. The longer you can leave meat in a yogurt marinade, the more tender it becomes.

Homemade lamb sausages in prosciutto

You don't need any fancy equipment or ingredients to make your own sausages. I wrap minced lamb in slices of delicious prosciutto for my moist, spicy bangers. Try making these in a smaller, slimmer size and serving as a canapé, with a minted cucumber and yogurt dip.

Serves 4 (makes 12 sausages)
Preparation time 15–20 minutes
Cooking time 20–25 minutes
Can be made in advance to end of step 3

500g (1lb 2oz) minced lamb
1 tbsp ground coriander
2 tbsp ground cumin
½ red onion, finely chopped
3 tbsp chopped parsley
1 chilli, deseeded and finely chopped
4 tbsp breadcrumbs
1 free-range egg, beaten
salt flakes and black pepper
12 slices prosciutto
olive oil, for the baking sheet

1 Preheat the oven to 190°C/375°F/gas mark 5.

2 Place the lamb in a large mixing bowl and break up a little with a fork. Add the coriander, cumin, onion, parsley, chilli and breadcrumbs, mix thoroughly, then add the egg. Season very well.

3 Divide the mixture into 12 equal-sized balls. With wet hands, shape these into sausages (*see* secret, page 24). Tightly wrap each sausage in a slice of prosciutto, leaving both ends open.

4 Place the sausages on a lightly oiled baking sheet, and bake for 20–25 minutes, or until golden brown and cooked through.

The best minced meat
Once mince oxidises it turns dull brown, so avoid buying any that doesn't have a healthy reddish tone as this shows its age. I always try to buy lean mince. If you're feeling super-virtuous, mince meat yourself (though I never do!) so you'll know exactly what's in it, including how much fat. Many food processors come with a mincing attachment (you'll find it at the bottom of your dustiest kitchen cupboard), or you can simply chop meat in the food processor.

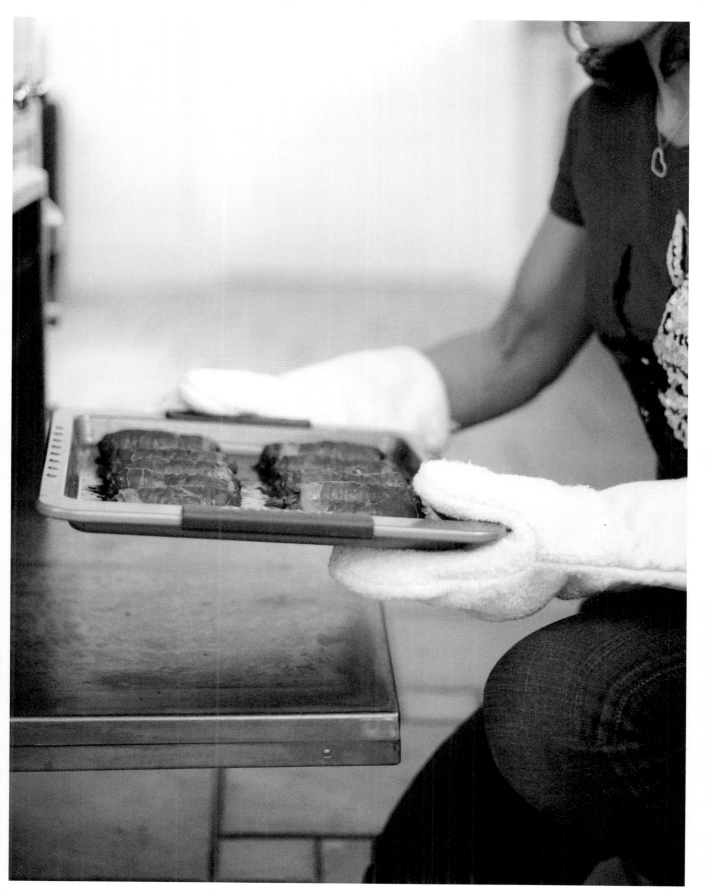

Lamb kidneys in cream & mushroom sauce

When I was a child, my mother used to serve this to us on toast. It's a great way to encourage children to eat kidneys. My mother was way ahead of her time, as these days offal of all sorts is the height of culinary fashion in the best restaurants.

Serves 2
Preparation time 10 minutes
Cooking time 15 minutes

275g (9¾oz) lamb kidneys, trimmed
   (*see* secret, below)
salt flakes and black pepper
2 tbsp plain flour, to dust
1 tbsp olive oil
25g (1oz) unsalted butter
2 shallots, finely chopped
100g (3½oz) mushrooms, roughly chopped
150ml (5fl oz) dry white wine
150ml (5fl oz) chicken stock
75ml (2½fl oz) double cream
1 heaped tsp grain mustard
2 tbsp chopped flatleaf parsley
2 thick slices wholemeal bread

1 Cut the kidneys into 2cm (¾in) chunks and season generously, then sprinkle over the flour and toss to coat evenly. Pour the oil into a frying pan and place over a high heat until smoking. Add the kidneys to the pan, being careful to avoid splashes. Keep a close eye on them, turning so they colour all over but don't burn, then remove them to a bowl. They should be sealed but not cooked through.

2 Place the butter in the pan over a medium heat and, when it has melted, add the shallots. Sauté for 2–3 minutes, or until softened. Add the mushrooms and continue to cook for 3 minutes.

3 Pour in the white wine and boil until the liquid has reduced by two-thirds. Pour in the stock and allow it to reduce by half, then add the cream and any juices from the bottom of the bowl of kidneys. Allow the sauce to bubble gently and thicken, then add the mustard. Reduce the heat now so the contents of the pan are no longer bubbling or the mixture will split.

4 Transfer the kidneys back into the pan and stir to coat in the sauce and cook through. Add the parsley and cook, stirring, for 5 minutes. Meanwhile, toast the bread. Serve the kidneys on the toast with sauce.

How to trim kidneys

Of course, you can get your butcher to trim kidneys, but sometimes – and especially if you shop at farmers' markets – you will have to buy them whole. Don't be discouraged! Simply peel off the membrane covering the kidneys, then, with a pair of scissors, cut them in half and trim out the tough white core from each piece. Never overcook kidneys or they go rubbery; make sure they remain succulently pink within.

Pork loin with pancetta & sage

This dish looks very fancy, wrapped in its pancetta jacket, but it's beautifully simple to make. Accompanied by wet polenta and a dressed rocket salad, it is smart enough to serve at any supper party. Or have it as a romantic meal for two; any leftovers are wonderful cold.

Serves 4
Preparation time 10 minutes
Cooking time 30 minutes
Can be made in advance to end of step 3
Suitable for freezing

12 pancetta strips
salt flakes and black pepper
12 small sage leaves
325g (11½oz) piece pork tenderloin
1 tbsp olive oil

1 Preheat the oven to 180°C/350°F/gas mark 4.

2 Cover the surface of your chopping board with a layer of clingfilm, then lay on the pancetta strips, slightly overlapping each other. Season well with pepper, then put a sage leaf on each strip. Place the pork on top, at a right angle to the pancetta strips, season, then lift up the clingfilm to roll the loin in pancetta. Remove the clingfilm.

3 Tear a piece of foil big enough to wrap the loin and season the foil. Place the pork on the foil, then turn it through the seasoning. Tightly roll up the foil around the meat and seal it so the shape resembles a cracker, twisting each end. Cut off any excess foil.

4 Place the foil parcel in the oven for 15 minutes, then remove and set aside until cool enough to handle. Turn the oven up to 200°C/400°F/gas mark 6.

5 Remove the foil, place the loin on a baking sheet and sprinkle with oil. Return it to the oven for 10 minutes, or until the loin is cooked through and the pancetta is crisp.

Making pork loin juicy

Pork tenderloin is a relatively expensive cut, as it is very lean. However, being lean also makes it prone to drying out and turning to dust in the mouth unless treated with care. Wrapping the loin in pancetta, as in this recipe, will solve the problem and result in succulent, juicy meat. Bacon does the same job, if you can't find pancetta.

Pork chops with honey & mustard glaze

This recipe features steamed vegetables. Steaming is a really healthy way of cooking as you don't lose the nutrients or flavour that you do when boiling vegetables. The honey and mustard glaze would be equally good spread over baby back ribs of pork, which are popular with my children.

Serves 4
Preparation time 5 minutes
Cooking time 30 minutes

salt flakes and black pepper
4 pork chops
1 tbsp olive oil
200g (7oz) purple-sprouting or
    Tenderstem broccoli, trimmed
1 tbsp chilli oil
1 garlic clove, finely chopped
1 chilli, deseeded and finely chopped
3 tbsp flaked almonds

For the honey & mustard glaze
3 tbsp Dijon mustard
2 tbsp runny honey
2 tsp soy sauce

1 Preheat the oven to 190°C/375°F/gas mark 5.

2 For the honey and mustard glaze, mix together all the ingredients with a pinch of salt in a small bowl.

3 Season both sides of the pork chops. Pour the olive oil into a large frying pan over a high heat, add the chops and cook for 2–3 minutes on each side, until lightly golden brown. Lay the chops on a baking sheet and spread on the honey and mustard topping, then bake for 25 minutes. To ensure they are cooked through, remove a chop from the oven and slice it through with a sharp knife. If any trace of pink remains inside, return to the oven for 2–3 minutes more, then test again.

4 Meanwhile, bring a pan of water that fits your steamer to the boil and set up the steamer above it. Add the broccoli, cover and cook for 4–5 minutes, or until tender. Heat the chilli oil in a frying pan or wok over a medium heat, then toss in the garlic, chilli and almonds and cook for 3–4 minutes, stirring, until toasted. Add the broccoli and stir to coat in the aromatics and almonds. Serve immediately alongside the chops.

Preparing a pork chop
Using a sharp pair of scissors or sharp knife, snip through the rind and fat at 2.5cm (1in) intervals along the length of each chop. This will prevent it from curling up during cooking.

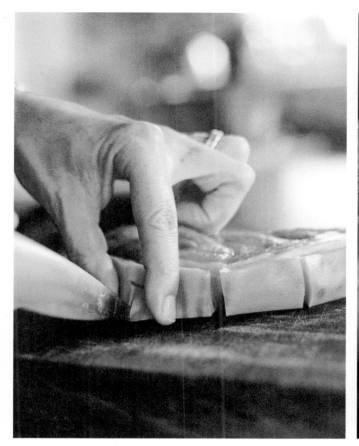

Simple pork stir-fry

You can use whatever vegetables you like in this recipe; it's a handy way to finish up any odds and ends that you may have knocking about in the fridge.

Serves 4
Preparation time 15 minutes
Cooking time 10 minutes

2 tbsp plain flour
salt flakes and black pepper
600g (1lb 5oz) pork tenderloin,
    thinly sliced
2 tbsp olive oil
3 carrots, cut into thin batons
1 red pepper, deseeded and thinly sliced
1 green pepper, deseeded and
    thinly sliced
24 French beans, trimmed
20 baby button mushrooms
juice of 1 lemon
generous splash of soy sauce
3 tsp Thai fish sauce
500g (1lb 2oz) fresh egg noodles

1 Put the flour into a resealable food bag, season very well and shake gently to mix. Add the pork, seal the bag and shake well to coat. Transfer to a sieve to remove any excess flour. Meanwhile, bring a large pan of salted water to the boil.

2 Pour the oil into a large frying pan or wok over a high heat, drop in the pork and stir for 1–2 minutes, until all sides are brown. Add the vegetables and toss, then pour in the lemon juice, soy sauce and fish sauce, and stir-fry for 5–10 minutes, until the vegetables are tender but still perky and the pork is cooked through. To test the pork, remove a piece to a saucer and slice it. There should be no trace of pink. If there is, continue to stir-fry for 1 minute, then test again.

3 Meanwhile, cook the noodles in boiling water as directed on the packet, then drain. Divide the noodles between 4 warmed plates and serve the pork and vegetables on the top.

How to make a stir-fry

Stir-frying is quick-cooking over a high heat using very little oil, while constantly moving the food around the pan. The most time-consuming part is preparing the ingredients: cut all vegetables to roughly the same size so they cook evenly. The exception to this is if you are using leaves, such as pak choi, which should be added just 3–4 minutes before the end of the cooking time so that they remain tender yet crisp rather than overcooked and soggy. Prepare all the vegetables in advance as there will be no spare time during cooking. If the pan seems dry during stir-frying, add a splash of water to help steam the vegetables and amalgamate all the flavourings.

Breaded veal escalopes with mozzarella & tomato & red pepper sauce

I was appearing on 'Hell's Kitchen' in the States as a contestant, in disguise so Gordon wouldn't recognise me. This is what I cooked: it's a favourite recipe of mine. If you can find the super-buttery burrata cheese, use it instead of mozzarella, though this is delicious either way.

Serves 2
Preparation time 40–45 minutes
Cooking time 30 minutes
Can be made in advance to end of step 4
Suitable for freezing (meat and sauce separately) at end of step 4

2 veal escalopes
125g (4½oz) breadcrumbs
1 tbsp dried oregano
25g (1oz) Parmesan cheese, finely grated
salt flakes and black pepper
1 free-range egg, beaten
2 tbsp plain flour
2 tbsp olive oil
juice of ¼ lemon
250g (9oz) buffalo mozzarella cheese
3 basil leaves, shredded

For the sauce
1 tbsp olive oil
3 shallots, finely chopped
2 garlic cloves, finely chopped
2 red chillies, deseeded and finely chopped
300g (10½oz) cherry tomatoes, halved
1 small yellow pepper, deseeded and
    thinly sliced
handful of basil leaves, finely chopped
2 tbsp Worcestershire sauce
splash of sherry vinegar

1 To make the sauce, pour the oil into a large frying pan over a medium heat, add the shallots, garlic and chillies and sauté for 2–3 minutes until softened but not coloured. Add the tomatoes, yellow pepper, basil and Worcestershire sauce, season and allow to cook gently for 15–20 minutes. Towards the end of cooking time, stir in the vinegar.

2 Remove the sauce from the heat, pour into a blender and process until smooth. You may have to do this in batches as the blender should be no more than half full each time to avoid an overspill; hold the lid on with a dish cloth to protect your hands from splashes. Set aside.

3 Flatten each piece of veal until 1cm (½in) thick (*see* secret, page 66).

4 Mix together the breadcrumbs, oregano and Parmesan and season. Spread this coating on a plate. Pour the egg on to a second plate and place the flour on a third. Season the flour very well and mix to combine. Place the three plates side by side. Coat the veal escalopes in the flour, shake off any excess, then turn through the egg, ensuring all surfaces are covered. Finally, press the veal into the breadcrumbs, coating both sides. If you have time, put the escalopes on a plate, cover and refrigerate for 30 minutes to help the coating to stick. Return to room temperature before continuing.

For the rocket salad
handful of rocket leaves
1 tbsp olive oil
½ tbsp aged balsamic vinegar

To serve
handful of Parmesan cheese shavings
2 lemon wedges

5 Place a large frying pan over a medium-high heat, pour in the oil and, when it is hot, add the veal and brown lightly on both sides. Reduce the temperature and cook slowly for 4–5 minutes. Squeeze over the lemon juice just before the end of cooking. Remove the escalopes from the pan and place on kitchen paper to blot off any excess oil.

6 Heat the grill to its highest setting. Pour the puréed sauce into a saucepan and gently reheat. Put the veal on to the grill pan. Slice the mozzarella into 6 and lay 3 slices on each escalope. Place under the hot grill and allow the cheese to melt, then scatter over the basil.

7 Meanwhile, place the rocket into a small bowl and pour in the oil and vinegar. Turn lightly with your hands to coat.

8 Put each escalope on to a warmed plate, spoon over the sauce and sprinkle with Parmesan shavings. Add a lemon wedge and serve with the dressed rocket salad.

Choosing happy veal

Buy 'rose' veal, which is ethically produced and has a pink colour. This way you can feel satisfied that the calves have been kept and slaughtered humanely. Avoid milk-fed veal, which produces a much paler meat: the standards of welfare for these animals are very poor.

Rump steak flavoured with anchovy & garlic

The flavours here complement one another beautifully; this is a wonderfully different way of cooking great steak. It's so good I'd eat it twice a week if I could! The steak I used was more or less 2.5cm (1in) thick, and the timings here will produce a medium-rare steak. This is fantastic served with a crisp, green salad or grilled vine tomatoes.

Serves 1
Preparation time 5 minutes,
   plus 1–2 hours marinating
Cooking time 5 minutes

280g (10oz) rump steak
3 canned anchovy fillets in olive oil
2 garlic cloves, very finely sliced

The perfect steak

Start with your meat at room temperature and make sure your pan is red-hot; if it's too cool, the steak will be tough. Turn the steak only once during cooking. It's impossible to generalise about how long to cook it, as that depends on the size, cut and thickness of your meat. Instead, prod it! A rare steak will feel soft; well-done will feel firm; medium will be somewhere in between the two. Rest the steak for 5 minutes before serving.

1 Using a small, sharp knife, make about 10 slits all the way through the steak.

2 Drain the anchovies, reserving their oil, and slice into 2.5cm (1in) pieces. Press a piece of anchovy and a slice of garlic into each slit on the steak. Pour the anchovy oil over the top of the steak and rub it in. Cover with clingfilm and leave to marinate in the refrigerator for 1–2 hours, removing 30 minutes before cooking as the meat should be cooked from room temperature.

3 Heat a nonstick frying pan over a high heat. When it is smoking, lay in the steak. Allow it to colour nicely on the underside for about 2 minutes. Turn it over and cook for a further 2–3 minutes (*see* secret, left, for tips on knowing when your steak is done to your liking). Tip the pan so the fat crisps and colours as well.

4 Place the steak on a warmed plate and allow to rest for 5 minutes before serving.

Spicy chicken wings

This recipe's harshest critic is my 9-year-old son. A favourite local restaurant of his apparently does 'the best'; mine are second best... But this is a marvellous recipe and easy to have on the table in a trice. Supply lots of kitchen paper for the inevitable mess!

Serves 4
Preparation time 5–10 minutes,
    plus 2–24 hours marinating
Cooking time 20–25 minutes
Can be made in advance to end of step 1
Suitable for freezing at end of step 1

6 tbsp hoisin sauce
2 tbsp sesame oil
4 tbsp runny honey
3 tbsp hot chilli sauce
2 tbsp dark soy sauce
2 tbsp grain mustard
24 chicken wings

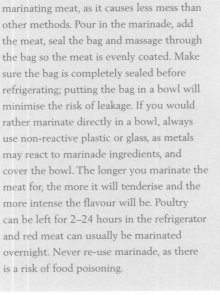

Marinating meat

I use a resealable food bag for marinating meat, as it causes less mess than other methods. Pour in the marinade, add the meat, seal the bag and massage through the bag so the meat is evenly coated. Make sure the bag is completely sealed before refrigerating; putting the bag in a bowl will minimise the risk of leakage. If you would rather marinate directly in a bowl, always use non-reactive plastic or glass, as metals may react to marinade ingredients, and cover the bowl. The longer you marinate the meat for, the more it will tenderise and the more intense the flavour will be. Poultry can be left for 2–24 hours in the refrigerator and red meat can usually be marinated overnight. Never re-use marinade, as there is a risk of food poisoning.

1 Place all the ingredients except the chicken in a large bowl and mix thoroughly, then transfer to a large resealable food bag. Add the chicken wings, seal the bag and turn, massaging the wings to make sure they are completely covered with a generous amount of marinade (*see* secret, below left). Ensure the bag is well sealed, put it into a large bowl and place in the refrigerator to marinate for between 2 and 24 hours.

2 Remove the chicken from the refrigerator and bring to room temperature. Meanwhile, preheat the oven to 220°C/425°F/gas mark 7.

3 Space out the wings on an oven tray lined with greaseproof paper and cook in the oven for 20–25 minutes, until deliciously crispy and sticky, turning once. To test they're done, pierce a wing through the thickest part right to the bone with a small, sharp knife. The juices should run clear; if there is any trace of pink, return to the oven for a couple of minutes, then test again.

4 Watch your fingers, as the chicken wings will be very hot and you won't resist them for long!

Marinated duck breasts

These are lovely for a romantic meal. Unlike chicken, duck can be served rare and juicy if you like. The cooking time I give here will produce beautifully juicy, medium duck breasts. If you prefer yours well done, continue to cook them for a few minutes more on each side.

Serves 2
Preparation time 5–10 minutes,
    plus 30 minutes–24 hours marinating
Cooking time 15 minutes

2 × 140g (5oz) skinless duck breasts
dash of olive oil

For the marinade
2.5cm (1in) fresh root ginger, peeled and
    sliced lengthways
2 garlic cloves, halved lengthways
6 tbsp soy sauce
2 tbsp toasted sesame oil
1 tbsp runny honey

1 Mix together all the marinade ingredients and pour into a shallow dish. Lay the duck breasts into the marinade and turn to coat, then cover with clingfilm and leave to marinate at room temperature for 30 minutes, or in the refrigerator for up to 24 hours.

2 Remove from the marinade; reserve the liquid. Put the oil in a nonstick frying pan over a medium-high heat. Once it is hot, add the duck and cook for 2–3 minutes on each side, until caramelised (make sure the heat is not too high or the honey will burn). Add the marinade and allow it to bubble and thicken. Continue to cook for 5–10 minutes, turning occasionally. This will produce a medium-rare duck breast. If the marinade is too syrupy, add a splash of hot water to dilute.

3 Remove the duck from the heat and allow to rest for 5 minutes, then slice. Serve with the sauce spooned over.

Preparing duck breasts

I use skinless duck for this recipe, but often you'll want to serve it with skin and fat intact. With a sharp knife, trim off excess fat. Score the skin (but don't penetrate the flesh unless you are going to marinate the duck before cooking) to allow the fat to run out. Season and place skin-side down into a hot, dry, nonstick frying pan. Cook until the skin is crisp, then turn to cook the other side.

Chinese duck breast wraps

I used to make this with Chinese pancakes, which are delicious but can be hard to find. So now I use lettuce, which results in a lighter, healthier dish. To make this as a canapé, use baby Little Gem leaves as a 'cup' for the duck and slice the breast widthways.

Serves 4
Preparation time 20 minutes, plus
   30 minutes or overnight marinating
Cooking time 25 minutes
Sauce can be made in advance (*see* step 4)

pinch of salt
4 tbsp runny honey
3 tbsp soy sauce
1 tsp ground star anise
4 duck breasts, skin on
½ cucumber, deseeded and cut into batons
8 spring onions, cut into fine batons
12 large Iceberg lettuce leaves

For the sauce
400g can chopped tomatoes
4 tbsp hoisin sauce
few drops of chilli sauce
4 garlic cloves, crushed
4 tbsp soy sauce
2 tbsp rice wine vinegar
2 tsp ground coriander
1 tsp ground cinnamon
½ tsp Chinese five spice

1 Mix together the salt, honey, soy sauce and star anise and pour into a shallow dish.

2 Lay the duck breasts on a board, skin-side up. Make slits widthways across each breast about 1cm (½in) apart, deep enough to cut through the skin and fat and penetrate the flesh. Place the duck into the marinade and turn to coat, then cover with clingfilm and place in the refrigerator for at least 30 minutes or overnight. The flavour will improve the longer you leave them.

3 Preheat the oven to 190°C/375°F/gas mark 5.

4 Place all the ingredients for the sauce into a pan, set over a medium heat until it bubbles, then reduce the heat and leave to simmer for 10 minutes. Allow to cool, pour into a bowl, cover and set aside. The sauce will keep for up to 10 days in the fridge, but make sure it comes to room temperature before you use it.

5 Place a nonstick frying pan over a high heat. Add the duck breasts, skin-side down, and allow them to sear and render their fat for about 4 minutes. Turn and cook the flesh side for another 4 minutes, then place the duck on a baking sheet and cook in the oven for 15 minutes. Remove and allow to rest for 10 minutes (*see* secret, left).

6 Slice each duck breast lengthways, as thinly as you can, into long strips. Serve each sliced breast on the side of a warmed plate and provide the sauce, cucumber, spring onions and lettuce on the table, allowing guests to roll their own wraps.

Meat and heat

Never take meat straight from the refrigerator, cook and serve it instantly – the outside will overcook before the centre heats up. Take it out of the fridge at least 20 minutes before cooking (up to 1 hour for larger joints). After cooking, rest meat for at least 10 minutes; it becomes far more succulent. Large joints will need 20–30 minutes, insulated with foil.

Turkey escalopes with mashed butternut squash & corn on the cob

Turkey is very lean, and it's cheap as well. It is wonderful for all those people who only really enjoy eating white meat, as it has tons of flavour. Pick some up next time you're at the supermarket and see for yourself.

Serves 4
Preparation time 15 minutes
Cooking time 30 minutes

2 cobs of sweetcorn
drizzle of olive oil, ideally lemon-infused
8 × 1cm (½in) thick turkey escalopes
   (*see* secret, below)
2 tsp butter

For the mash
2 tbsp olive oil
1 butternut squash, peeled and diced
2 rosemary sprigs
1 garlic clove, finely chopped
knob of butter
salt flakes and black pepper
2 tbsp crème fraîche
dash of milk

1 Preheat the oven to 190°C/375°F/gas mark 5.

2 Begin with the mash. Drizzle the oil in a roasting tin and add the squash, rosemary, garlic and butter and season. Roast for 25 minutes, or until the squash is tender.

3 Meanwhile, bring a large saucepan of salted water to the boil over a high heat. Halve each cob of corn widthways and insert wooden skewers into both ends of each piece. Add the corn to the boiling water and cook for 8 minutes, or until tender.

4 Pour the oil for the escalopes into a frying pan and place over a high heat until hot. Season both sides of the turkey pieces and fry for just 2 minutes each side. Check they are cooked by removing an escalope to a plate and slicing it through; if any trace of pink remains inside, place in the pan for 30 seconds more, then test again.

5 Remove the squash from the oven and discard the rosemary. Transfer the squash into a mixing bowl and add the crème fraîche and milk. Mash until smooth, then taste and adjust the seasoning, cover with foil and keep warm in a low oven.

6 Serve the turkey on warmed plates with a spoonful of mash and a piece of corn on the cob, each with a knob of butter melting over the top.

Bashing out escalopes
Place the meat pieces between 2 sheets of clingfilm on a work surface. Gently bash with a rolling pin or meat mallet until they are about 1cm (½in) thick. The clingfilm will prevent the meat from tearing, protect your work surface and keep the process hygienic.

Turkey masala kebabs

A lot of people overcook turkey, and therefore have the mistaken impression that it's a dry meat. It isn't; it's juicy and has a great depth of flavour. Just pay attention and cook it as carefully as you would any other lean meat. You will need 8 skewers for these kebabs.

Serves 4 (makes 8)
Preparation time 10 minutes,
   plus 15 minutes or overnight marinating
Cooking time 20 minutes
Can be made in advance to end of step 3

650g (1lb 7oz) turkey breast, diced
3 tbsp masala curry paste
16 large closed-cup mushrooms,
   stalks removed
1 red pepper, deseeded and cut into
   2.5cm (1in) dice
1 yellow pepper, deseeded and cut into
   2.5cm (1in) dice
1 red onion, cut into 2.5cm (1in) chunks
1 large courgette, cut into 2.5cm (1in) rounds
3 tbsp olive oil

1 Preheat the oven to 200°C/400°F/gas mark 6.

2 Place the turkey in a mixing bowl, spoon in the curry paste and stir to coat. Cover with clingfilm and leave to marinate for 15 minutes at room temperature, or overnight in the refrigerator if you are organised enough!

3 Arrange all the vegetables in bowls. Thread a mushroom on to each skewer, then alternate the turkey and other vegetables. Finish off with another mushroom.

4 Put the kebabs on a baking sheet, place in the oven and cook for 10 minutes, then turn over and cook for 10 minutes more, or until the turkey is cooked through. Check a piece of meat by slicing it through; if any trace of pink remains inside, return to the oven for a minute more, then test again.

5 Serve the kebabs on warmed plates, allowing 2 skewers per person.

Talking diced turkey

Readily available, lean and inexpensive, turkey should not be saved only for Christmas! Most diced turkey you can buy is breast meat, which has a tendency to be dry because it contains almost no fat. Although the meat must always be fully cooked through for safety – as is the case with chicken – you should take care to avoid overcooking as dry turkey has an unpleasant, dusty texture.

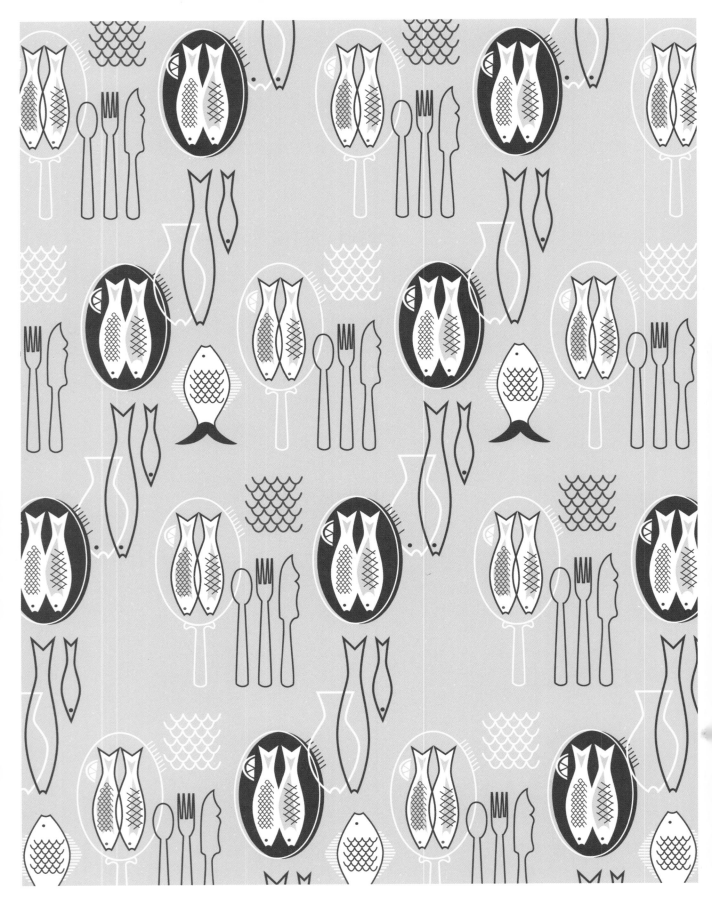

Fish

Moroccan fish tagine · Salmon fillet in black sauce · Spanish fish soup

Pollack & prawn pie with smoked paprika mash

Salt-baked sea bream · Grilled tuna & vegetable kebabs

Seared coriander-crusted tuna steaks with miso

Smoked haddock fishcakes · Thai red curry

Crab & sweetcorn soup · Sautéed calamari with chorizo & peppers

Mussels with Belgian beer

Secrets of cooking fish

With fish and shellfish, timings are vital as you must never overcook them. Poaching is a really good way to start off if you're new to fish cookery. You'll know the fish is ready when you can gently flake the flesh with a fork.

It's impressive to cook a whole fish. I learned how to salt-bake fish (*see* page 82) when I was presenting a TV cooking show, and it is among the most eye-popping dishes to bring to the table when you have friends for dinner.

Try cooking fillets of fish *en papillote*: place them on a large square of greaseproof paper, then add the seasonings you like, such as lemon or herbs, and a knob of butter. Seal the greaseproof paper into a parcel around the fish and bake until you can gently flake the flesh. When you open the package at the table, you will get a fantastic waft of fragrances.

People get scared of shellfish but, if you follow my simple tips – for instance, in my Mussels with Belgian Beer (*see* page 98) – you will quickly learn that it's easy to cook them safely. And they are super-speedy: you don't have to do a lot with them.

With careful shopping, ready-cooked fish can make an instant starter. Buy prawns for a cocktail and serve with my Tomato & Tarragon Mayonnaise (*see* page 272) for a new twist on an old favourite. Dressed crab is always impressive. Or, if you're feeling flush, try a lobster roll with rocket and mayonnaise for a near-instant treat.

Though fish needs exact timings, don't be put off. The base for my Thai Red Curry (*see* page 92) can be made the day before; in fact it improves with reheating, so makes a quick and easy supper.

It's good to know how to make a comforting fish pie (*see* page 78). You can use cheap, sustainable fish such as pollack, and hide a multitude of vegetables from the children in the sauce! My recipe has a delicious paprika mash, but it's also nice topped with puff pastry. After a recent half-marathon I had three helpings.

Fish is wonderfully good for you. We have it once or twice a week and always make a point of eating oily fish such as salmon. I stick to the rule of fish on a Friday, which was the way it was at my school.

Moroccan fish tagine

I make this simple tagine for the children, taking care not to add too much salt. The lemon compensates for the lack of salt and works well with the peppers and tomatoes. When cooking this for adults, I fry two merguez sausages, cut them into chunks, along with the peppers, and sprinkle in 2 tablespoons rinsed capers before baking.

Serves 6
Preparation time 10 minutes,
    plus 30 minutes marinating
Cooking time 35 minutes
Can be made in advance to end of step 4

3 garlic cloves, crushed
2 tsp ground cumin
3 tsp paprika
3 tbsp tomato purée
6 tbsp lemon juice
6 × 150g (5½oz) monkfish fillets, skinned
1 tbsp olive oil
2 red peppers, deseeded and cut into
    2cm (¾in) dice
15 cherry tomatoes, sliced
salt flakes and black pepper
small handful of coriander leaves, chopped

Adding flavour to fish
Marinating fish is easy. Simply mix your chosen acid ingredients (such as lemon juice or vinegar) with oils (such as extra-virgin olive oil), seasonings and herbs and pour them over the fish in a non-reactive glass or plastic bowl before refrigerating for 20–30 minutes. Be careful not to leave it any longer or the acids will start to 'cook' the fish, producing a mushy result.

1 In a non-reactive glass or plastic bowl, mix together the garlic, cumin, paprika, tomato purée and lemon juice. Put the monkfish into the bowl, rub it all over with the spice mixture, then cover with clingfilm. Leave to marinate in the refrigerator for 30 minutes.

2 Preheat the oven to 190°C/375°F/gas mark 5.

3 Heat a nonstick frying pan over a medium heat, pour in the oil, add the peppers and cook, stirring, for 2–3 minutes until softened.

4 Lay half the tomatoes and cooked peppers in an ovenproof dish and arrange the monkfish fillets on top. Scatter with the remaining tomatoes and peppers. Season and cover the dish with foil.

5 Bake for 25–30 minutes, or until the fish is firm and cooked through. To test, firmly press a fillet with the back of a fork. It should start to break into opaque flakes. If it looks translucent inside, cook for 2–3 minutes more before testing again.

6 Sprinkle the tagine with the coriander and serve on a bed of basmati rice or butternut squash mash (*see* page 66).

Salmon fillet in black sauce

This dish is delicious served with mangetouts and wild rice. The crunchiness of the vegetables and nutty quality of the rice really complement the strong, salty-sweet flavours of the glaze on the moist fish. And this is one of the easiest recipes in the whole book!

Serves 2
Preparation time 5 minutes
Cooking time 15 minutes

4 tbsp soy sauce
2 tbsp sesame oil
2 tbsp runny honey
500g (1lb 2oz) skinless salmon fillet,
    cut into 2 pieces

1 Preheat the oven to 180°C/350°F/gas mark 4.

2 Mix together the soy sauce, sesame oil and honey in a small bowl. Place the salmon fillets on a baking sheet, spoon over the marinade and gently rub it into the top of the fish. Cook in the oven for 10–15 minutes, removing occasionally to spoon the sauce back over the salmon.

3 Remove from the oven and allow to rest for 5 minutes, then serve drizzled with any of the marinade that remains on the baking sheet.

How to skin a piece of fish

If you buy salmon with the skin on, don't panic! It's easy to remove. Place the salmon skin-side down on a board. Take hold of one corner and insert a fine knife blade – ideally a filleting knife as the blade is flexible – between skin and flesh. Firmly grab the corner of the skin and, using a zig-zag motion, slice the skin away from the flesh, keeping the knife as close to the skin as you can.

Spanish fish soup

Any flaky white fish would be excellent in this soup; I have chosen whiting as it is inexpensive. Ask your fishmonger what's best, and of course be guided by what is cheap and sustainable; the two usually go hand in hand.

Serves 4
Preparation time 15 minutes
Cooking time 25 minutes

60g (2¼oz) chorizo sausage, roughly chopped
2 tbsp olive oil
1 Spanish onion, roughly chopped
3 garlic cloves, left whole
1 red pepper, deseeded and finely sliced
500g (1lb 2oz) whiting, or other flaky white
   fish, skinned and chopped into chunks
350g (12oz) flavoursome tomatoes,
   roughly chopped
500ml (18fl oz) chicken stock (*see* secret,
   page 37), plus extra to adjust consistency
1 tsp smoked paprika
salt flakes and black pepper

1 Place a dry frying pan over a medium heat, add the chorizo and fry until it releases its oil and begins to turn crispy. Set aside.

2 Heat the olive oil in a large pan over a medium heat. Add the onion and garlic cloves and fry for 6–8 minutes until the onion is soft.

3 Add the red pepper to the onion and gently fry until it softens, too. Add the fish, tomatoes, stock and smoked paprika and leave these to cook for 15 minutes. Season to taste.

4 Ladle the soup into a blender and process until smooth. You may have to do this in batches as the blender should be no more than half full each time to avoid an overspill; hold the lid on with a dish cloth to protect your hands from splashes.

5 Return the soup to a clean pan and place over a gentle heat to reheat before serving, adding enough extra stock or water to bring it to a consistency you like. Pour the soup into warmed bowls, sprinkle the crispy chorizo on top then drizzle the surface of each portion with the chorizo oil.

Pork and fish: perfect partners

Although it's not common in this country beyond the Welsh dish of cockles with bacon, mixing pork with fish is a popular custom among the Spanish and Portuguese. It's an excellent combination, with the succulence of the meat giving an extra dimension to the seafood. Extend the idea and try cold oysters served with hot, spicy sausages, seared scallops with black pudding, pork with clams or herrings in oatmeal fried with bacon.

Pollack & prawn pie with smoked paprika mash

This recipe isn't a traditional fish pie, but I find the tomatoes really intensify in flavour as they bake, complementing the dish perfectly along with the smoked paprika and cayenne pepper. My fishmonger first tipped me off about pollack. It's relatively cheap, sustainable and excellently meaty; ideal for a pie. Use another flaky white fish if pollack is unavailable.

Serves 4–6
Preparation time 20–25 minutes
Cooking time 50 minutes
Can be made in advance

600g (1lb 5oz) pollack fillet or other flaky
   white fish, skin on
500g (1lb 2oz) raw tiger prawns,
   shelled and deveined
600ml (1 pint) milk
2 bay leaves
6 peppercorns
few parsley stalks
drizzle of olive oil
1 large leek, finely chopped
100g (3½oz) pancetta, cubed
50g (1¾oz) butter
50g (1¾oz) flour
2 tbsp finely chopped parsley
1 tbsp finely chopped basil

For the topping
1.5kg (3lb 5oz) Maris Piper potatoes,
   cut into even chunks
pinch of salt
knob of butter
splash of milk
1½ tsp smoked paprika
pinch of cayenne pepper
2 free-range egg yolks
160g (5¾oz) cherry tomatoes, halved
2 tsp thyme leaves

1 Begin with the topping. Place the potatoes in a pan of cold water, add the salt and bring to the boil, then reduce the heat and simmer for 15 minutes, until tender. Drain very well (*see* secret, page 20). Add the butter and milk and mash until smooth. Stir in the paprika and cayenne pepper, then stir in the egg yolks. Set aside.

2 Put the pollack and prawns into a deep pan and add enough of the milk just to cover, then pop in the bay leaves, peppercorns and parsley stalks. Place over a medium heat and let it come to a bubble, then turn off the heat, cover with foil or a lid and leave to cook in the residual heat for 10–15 minutes. Using a slotted spoon, remove the fish and prawns from the milk. Strain the milk through a sieve into a bowl and set aside. Flake the fish on to a plate, removing the skin and any bones.

3 Heat the oil in a pan and gently fry the leek and pancetta for 2–3 minutes. Remove from the heat and set aside.

4 Preheat the oven to 190°C/375°F/gas mark 5. Melt the 50g (1¾oz) butter in a saucepan, add the flour and mix to form a thick paste. Whisk in the reserved milk from poaching the fish and prawns, a little at a time to avoid lumps, until it is all incorporated. Cook for 4–5 minutes, still whisking occasionally, until the sauce is smooth and thick enough to coat the back of a spoon. Stir in the chopped parsley and basil.

Go for sustainable fish

I would like my children to enjoy fish all
their lives, as I have, so I always try to buy
varieties from stocks that aren't endangered.
Pollack is an excellent example of this, and
is very underused; its white, meaty and flaky
flesh is perfect for this recipe. If you can't
find it, you can use cod instead, but make
sure you buy farmed cod so you can tuck in
with a clear conscience.

5 Put the pollack and prawns in a 2.5-litre
(4½-pint) ovenproof dish along with the leeks
and pancetta, evenly distributing these ingredients
over the bottom of the dish so each serving will
have some of everything. Pour in the white sauce
and gently stir it through.

6 Spread the mash over the top and smooth with
the back of a fork. Arrange the halved tomatoes
on top and very gently push them slightly into the
mash. Sprinkle on the thyme leaves and cook in
the oven for 30 minutes, until bubbling and golden.

Salt-baked sea bream

I had seen fish cooked in this way several times and had always been intrigued, so I came up with this recipe. The fish is steamed in the salt that is packed around it and, when cooked, the flesh is incredibly moist and delicate. Give it a go! This dish is delicious served with steamed broccoli and new potatoes.

Serves 2
Preparation time 10 minutes
Cooking time 25 minutes

1.5kg (3lb 5oz) coarse sea salt
3 free-range egg whites
2 × 450g (1lb) sea bream, or other
   small-medium, deep-bodied white fish,
   gutted and scaled
1 unwaxed lemon, sliced
few rosemary or thyme sprigs

1 Preheat the oven to 200°C/400°F/gas mark 6.

2 Place the sea salt in a large bowl, add the egg whites and stir them in. Take a large baking tin and pour on a 1½cm (¾in) bed of the salt mixture. Lay the two fish on top so they face top to tail. Insert the lemon slices and herbs into the cavities of each. Close the cavities and pack over a second layer of the salt mixture, again about 1½cm (¾in) thick (*see* secret, below left).

3 Place in the oven for 20–25 minutes until cooked (*see* secret, below left).

4 Remove the top layer of salt and take out the fish. Remove the heads and skin and serve. Alternatively, just place the dish in the middle of the table with a flourish and dig in!

Salt-baking fish
Pick the freshest fish you can find and stuff it with your preferred aromatics; try fennel, orange or dill. A large fish cooked in this way makes a great centrepiece for the table; take it to the table with the crust cracked and let guests help themselves. You must make sure the fish is entirely encased in the salt mixture as you don't want the fish juices to leak. It is cooked when a firm tap will crack the salty crust.

Grilled tuna & vegetable kebabs

You will need 8 wooden skewers for these kebabs: always pre-soak them in a deep bowl of water for at least 10 minutes before use to prevent burning. Choose sustainable line-caught tuna and serve with fluffy basmati rice, or opt for the lettuce bed recipe here for a lighter option.

Serves 4
Preparation time 10 minutes
Cooking time 20–25 minutes
Can be made in advance to end of step 2

1 red onion, cut into 8 wedges
1 yellow pepper, deseeded and cut into
   3cm (1¼in) dice
1 courgette, cut into 3cm (1¼in) half-moons
2 tbsp olive oil, plus extra for the vegetables
4 × 140g (5oz) tuna steaks, cut into
   2.5cm (1in) dice
12 cherry vine tomatoes
salt flakes and black pepper
1 tsp dried parsley
1 tsp dried oregano
juice of 1 lime

For the lettuce bed (optional)
1 tbsp olive oil
2 baby Little Gem lettuces,
   quartered lengthways
1 tbsp balsamic vinegar
1 tsp sesame seeds

1 Preheat the oven to 180°C/350°F/gas mark 4. Put the onion, yellow pepper and courgette into a roasting dish and drizzle with a little oil. Toss with your hands so that everything is coated. Cook in the oven for 15 minutes, or until softened, then remove.

2 Heat the grill to its highest setting. Put the tuna into a bowl with the roasted vegetables and the tomatoes. Drizzle over the 2 tbsp oil, season and add the dried herbs. Toss together to coat with all the seasonings. Thread the ingredients on to the soaked skewers, evenly dividing the pieces of tuna and vegetables between them.

3 Place the kebabs in a grill pan and slide under the hot grill for 5–10 minutes, turning frequently. Just before they are ready, squeeze over the lime juice.

4 Meanwhile make the lettuce bed, if liked. Pour the oil into a large frying pan placed over a high heat, add the lettuce and stir until it very slightly browns at the edges. Add the vinegar and sesame seeds and stir. Serve the kebabs on the lettuce bed.

How to choose and cook tuna
When buying tuna, go for chunky steaks that have a bright, rich, translucent red colour (it should be about the same shade as raw beef). Never overcook tuna, as it will lose its moisture and delicate flavour and become dry and unappetising. Always remove it from the heat while it is still pink in the middle. To check, slice a piece and look inside.

Seared coriander-crusted tuna steaks with miso

This is a bit of a cheat's dish, using packet miso paste, but it's also healthy and tasty! Make sure the tuna is at room temperature before cooking, or the centre will take longer to reach the correct heat than the outside, while the outside overcooks and ruins the steak.

Serves 1 large portion, or 2 light lunches
Preparation time 15 minutes
Cooking time 10–15 minutes

1 tbsp finely crushed coriander seeds
1 tsp crushed salt flakes
240g (8½oz) tuna steak
1 tbsp olive oil
2 × 15g sachets miso soup paste
150g (5½oz) fresh noodles
1 tsp finely chopped fresh root ginger
1 red chilli, deseeded and finely sliced
 on the diagonal
2 spring onions, finely sliced on the diagonal
15g (½oz) purple basil, finely chopped
15g (½oz) coriander leaves
drizzle of sesame oil
1 lime, cut into wedges

1 Mix the crushed coriander and salt together, then transfer to a plate. Lay the tuna on top and push down gently, then turn over and coat the other side.

2 Pour the oil into a frying pan over a medium-high heat, add the tuna and cook for about 3 minutes on each side, until lightly golden. Remove from the heat and let the tuna rest in the pan for 5–10 minutes.

3 Meanwhile, put the miso paste into a pan and add 400ml (14fl oz) boiling water, mixing well. Place over a medium heat until bubbling. Add the noodles and reduce the heat to a simmer. Add the ginger, chilli, spring onions and purple basil.

4 Ladle the noodles and some of the soup into a large, shallow bowl. Slice the tuna and arrange on top of the noodles. Ladle more of the soup over and sprinkle with the coriander leaves and sesame oil. Serve immediately with the lime to squeeze over just before eating.

The mysteries of miso

Miso is a fermented paste of soya beans that is an essential ingredient of Japanese food. It makes a wonderful storecupboard ingredient as it's delicious and takes only seconds to mix. Try your own adaptations of the dish above, by adding spinach, baby sweetcorn or sugarsnap peas, but don't overcomplicate it as you want the fresh, clean taste of the soup itself to be the star. Miso doesn't need salt, so go easy on the seasoning.

Smoked haddock fishcakes

These fishcakes can be prepared ahead of time and chilled in the fridge until use. This will firm them up and prevent them from breaking while cooking. Use any other sustainable smoked flaky white fish if haddock is unavailable. To make the mash ultra-smooth, pass the cooked potato through a potato ricer, or push through a sieve.

Makes 16 small fishcakes
Preparation time 30 minutes,
   plus 30 minutes chilling
Cooking time 30 minutes
Can be made in advance to end of step 4
Suitable for freezing at end of step 4

400g (14oz) Maris Piper potatoes,
   cut into 2.5cm (1in) dice
salt flakes and black pepper
300ml (½ pint) milk
200g (7oz) smoked haddock or other
   flaky white fish fillets
1 bay leaf
3 tbsp olive oil
1 large onion, finely chopped
finely grated zest of 1 small unwaxed lemon
1 tsp paprika
125g (4½oz) breadcrumbs
2 tbsp finely chopped flatleaf parsley
4–6 tbsp plain flour
2 free-range eggs, beaten
3 tsp grain mustard
2 tbsp half-fat crème fraîche
200g (7oz) curly kale

1 Put the potatoes in a pan of lightly salted water, place over a high heat and bring to the boil. Reduce the heat, cover and simmer for 15–20 minutes, or until tender. Drain well and mash until smooth (*see* secret, page 20).

2 Pour the milk into a shallow sauté pan, add the haddock fillets and bay leaf, then season. Place over a low heat and bring to a simmer. Cook gently for 6–10 minutes, until the fish is separating into flakes. Carefully strain off and reserve the liquor and bay leaf, cover and set aside in the refrigerator. Flake the fish into a bowl, removing and discarding the skin and any small bones.

3 Meanwhile, pour 1 tbsp of the oil into a frying pan over a medium heat and gently fry together the onion, lemon zest and paprika for 4–5 minutes, until the onion is soft but not coloured. Place this in the bowl with the fish. Stir in the mashed potato and mix. Taste and adjust the seasoning. Form the mixture into 16 equal-sized balls, then slightly flatten them into fishcakes, each about 2cm (¾in) thick.

4 Mix together the breadcrumbs and parsley and season. Using the breadcrumbs, flour and eggs, coat the fishcakes in a breadcrumb crust (*see* secret, opposite, for how to do this). Once they are coated, cover the fishcakes with clingfilm and refrigerate for at least 30 minutes, longer if possible: ideally make them in the morning and refrigerate until supper.

5 Remove the fishcakes from the refrigerator and return to room temperature. Meanwhile, preheat the oven to 180°C/350°F/gas mark 4.

Applying a breadcrumb coating to fish or meat

Make sure you have four plates close to hand: one holding seasoned flour, another beaten egg and the third breadcrumbs. Leave the last empty. Dip the fishcakes, fish or meat into the flour, shake off the excess, then turn them through the egg. Lastly press all sides into the breadcrumbs. Put the coated item on the fourth plate. If you can, use just one hand for this process, to avoid getting too messy.

6 Pour the remaining oil into an ovenproof frying pan, place over a medium heat, then gently fry the fishcakes for 3–5 minutes on each side, until lovely and golden. Transfer the pan to the oven and cook for a further 10–15 minutes.

7 Bring a pan of water that fits your steamer to the boil over a high heat. While it comes to the boil, make the sauce. Heat the reserved liquor and bay leaf in a small saucepan over a medium heat. Whisk in the grain mustard, then add the crème fraîche and allow to foam. Reduce the heat and keep the sauce warm. Place the kale in a steamer over the boiling water, cover and cook for 6–8 minutes, until tender.

8 Serve the fishcakes on warmed plates with the curly kale and a large spoonful of the mustard sauce.

Thai red curry

This dish is equally delicious with chicken thighs instead of prawns; add them with the butternut squash. When using coconut milk, whisk it briskly with a fork in the can before using – this helps to stop it splitting.

Serves 4 for a children's supper
Preparation time 20 minutes
Cooking time 40 minutes
Can be made in advance to end of step 2

1 onion, quartered
1 garlic clove
3 tbsp red curry paste
1 tbsp groundnut oil
400g can chopped tomatoes
2 × 400ml cans coconut milk
250ml (9fl oz) good fish or chicken stock
400g (14oz) butternut squash, peeled and
    cut into 2cm (¾in) dice
150g (5½oz) sugarsnap peas
12 button mushrooms, halved
4 tbsp fish sauce, or to taste
salt flakes and black pepper
400g (14oz) raw prawns (I use king prawns),
    shelled and deveined
juice of 1 lime

For the steamed rice
200g (7oz) basmati rice
1 cardamom pod, crushed
1 star anise

1 Place the onion, garlic and curry paste into a food processor and blend to make a paste. If you have don't have a processor, finely chop the onion and garlic together and stir in the curry paste.

2 Pour the oil into a large, deep pan and place over a medium heat. When the oil is hot, add the paste with the tomatoes and cook for 5–10 minutes, stirring constantly. Add the coconut milk and stock and bring to a bubble, then reduce the heat and stir in the squash. Simmer for 10–15 minutes, or until the squash is tender. Add the sugarsnap peas and mushrooms, then gradually add the fish sauce: stir through about half, then taste and add more if you want. Season to taste.

3 Meanwhile, prepare the rice. Place it in a sieve and rinse under a cold tap. Shake off the water and place the rice in a saucepan. Add 300ml (½ pint) cold water, a little salt, the cardamom and star anise. Bring to the boil over a high heat and cook for 5 minutes. Cover with a tight-fitting lid, reduce the heat to its lowest setting and cook for 12–14 minutes. Turn off the heat and allow to steam, still covered, for a further 10 minutes.

4 Add the prawns to the curry and stir for up to 5 minutes, or until they are pink and cooked through. Check the seasoning and add lime juice to taste. Remove the cardamom and star anise from the rice and fluff it up with a fork.

5 Serve the curry on a bed of rice.

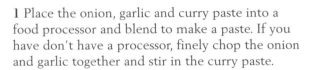

Preparing prawns

Prawns are sold fresh and frozen; make sure frozen prawns are thoroughly defrosted before cooking. Find and remove the black string that runs down their backs (it is a length of gut): run a small, sharp knife carefully down the back of the prawn, then use the knife to prise out the string.

Crab & sweetcorn soup

If fresh crab meat is not available, you can easily substitute tinned white crab meat in brine. I use frozen sweetcorn here as I find it much crunchier than canned when it's cooked, which gives a good, definite texture to this aromatic, unusual soup.

Serves 4
Preparation time 10–15 minutes
Cooking time 20 minutes

1.3 litres (2¼ pints) chicken stock
450g (1lb) frozen sweetcorn
4 spring onions, finely chopped
1cm (½in) fresh root ginger, peeled
    and finely chopped
1 tbsp Chinese rice wine
2–3 tsp soy sauce
1 tsp golden caster sugar
2 tsp cornflour
225g (8oz) cooked white crab meat
1 free-range egg white
1 tsp sesame oil
prawn crackers, to serve

1 Place the stock in a large pan and bring to the boil over a high heat. Add the sweetcorn, reduce the heat and allow to simmer for 10–15 minutes. Add the spring onions, ginger, rice wine, soy sauce and sugar. In a small bowl, mix the cornflour with just enough cold water to make a paste, then whisk this into the soup. Simmer gently, stirring, for 2–3 minutes, until the soup begins to thicken, then add the crab meat and stir.

2 In a small bowl, whisk together the egg white and sesame oil, then slowly pour this into the soup (make sure the soup is not boiling at this point), whisking constantly. It will form silky strands.

3 Serve the soup accompanied by prawn crackers.

Tackling a whole cooked crab

Lay the crab on its back and twist off the big claws. Pull the underside of the body from the top shell. You will see a circle of grey feathery gills – pull these off and discard them. Then, using a heavy knife, cut the body into four. This exposes tunnels containing the white meat. Pick it out with a skewer. Pull the knuckles from the large claws and pick out the meat. Place the large claws on a worktop and cover with a clean dish cloth. Smash with a rolling pin until the shell cracks, then extract the meat, discarding the thin blade within each claw. Spread out all the white crab meat on a broad plate and carefully pick through it with your fingers, discarding any bits of shell you find. Spoon the brown meat from the upper shell and keep it separate from the white meat. You do not need the brown meat for this dish, but it is delicious and great in soups, tarts, turnovers and pâtés.

Sautéed calamari with chorizo & peppers

I ate a dish similar to this one in South Africa and it was so delicious I invented my own version at home. My children had previously thought all calamari came in battered rings, but they love this. The chorizo complements the dish wonderfully (see secret, page 75).

Serves 4
Preparation time 20 minutes,
    plus 30 minutes marinating
Cooking time 10 minutes

900g (2lb) fresh calamari, cleaned and cut
    into 2cm (¾in) pieces (*see* secret, below)
300ml (½ pint) milk
1 tbsp olive oil
2 garlic cloves, finely chopped
1 chilli, deseeded and finely chopped
100g (3½oz) chorizo sausage, diced
400g (14oz) marinated peppers in oil,
    drained and sliced
juice of ½ lemon
1–2 tbsp plain flour
salt flakes and black pepper
2 handfuls of flatleaf parsley leaves,
    roughly chopped

1 Place the calamari into a shallow dish, pour in just enough milk to cover, cover in clingfilm and chill in the refrigerator for up to 30 minutes.

2 Heat the oil in a large, deep frying pan over a medium heat and sauté the garlic and chilli for 1 minute. Add the chorizo and continue to cook for a further 4–5 minutes, until it releases its oil. Add the peppers and stir for 3–4 minutes, then pour out any excess oil and add the lemon juice.

3 Meanwhile, remove the calamari from the milk and place on kitchen paper to absorb any excess moisture. Put the flour in a resealable food bag with plenty of seasoning, drop in the calamari, seal the bag and shake well to coat, then transfer to a sieve to remove any excess flour.

4 Add the calamari to the pan and continue to cook for just 1–2 minutes, stirring. Do not cook for any longer (*see* secret, below). Stir in the parsley, season to taste and serve immediately.

Tackling squid

You can usually buy squid already cleaned, but if yours aren't, don't worry. Working over a sink, pull the tentacles from the body and remove and discard the plastic-like tube (the quill) that emerges from inside, along with any intestines. Tear the fins from larger squid and peel off any mottled purple-brown skin. Cut off and discard the eyes and beak from below the tentacles. Rinse the pieces under cold water, then pat dry with kitchen paper. To tenderise squid, soak it in milk for up to 30 minutes, then either cook for the shortest possible time over a high heat or braise very slowly for more than 1 hour to break down the fibres.

Mussels with Belgian beer

Nothing is more associated with Belgium than mussels, so do the country justice and use their excellent beer in this recipe! A new twist on that old favourite moules marinière, this dish is best served with lots of crusty bread to soak up the fabulous juices.

Serves 2
Preparation time 10 minutes
Cooking time 10 minutes

500g (1lb 2oz) mussels
1 tbsp olive oil
100g (3½oz) pancetta, cubed
1 large leek, sliced into rings
2 thyme sprigs
330ml bottle Belgian beer

1 Clean the mussels and discard any that do not close when they are tapped on the side of the sink (*see* secret, below).

2 Pour the oil into a pan large enough to hold all the mussels and with a tight-fitting lid. Place it over a medium heat and gently fry the pancetta and leek for 2–3 minutes, then add the thyme and stir until everything is cooked through.

3 Tip in the mussels and add the beer. Place the lid on the pan and leave to steam for 5 minutes, or until the mussels are open. Discard any that remain closed. Serve immediately.

How to prepare mussels

Empty the mussels into the kitchen sink, then pull off the beard (the protruding scraps of hairs) from each shell. Scrub to clean and remove the worst of any barnacles. As you work, discard any mussels that are cracked, or that are open and do not close when tapped on the side of the sink (they may be dead). Rinse in fresh water. After cooking, discard any mussels that remain closed.

Pasta, rice & grains

Beef & aubergine rigatoni bake with tomato & basil
Anchovy, tomato & bacon pasta sauce · Pasta with bacon & vegetable sauce
Simple salmon, dill & crème fraîche pasta · Haddock & spring vegetable risotto
Chicken, lemon & rocket risotto · Red rice salad
Healthy couscous, my style

Secrets of cooking pasta, rice & grains

You must always have dried pasta in the cupboard for emergency suppers. We have spaghetti, linguine and lasagne sheets as well as shapes such as rigatoni for my Beef & Aubergine Rigatoni Bake with Tomato & Basil (*see* page 104).

Don't just reach for the sandwiches when children need a packed lunch. Pasta, tuna and sweetcorn provides a great lunchtime energy burst for them, as does a helping of the quite fabulous, nutty Red Rice Salad (*see* page 116), which is my mother's recipe.

Always make sure your storecupboard includes a couple of jars of pesto and your refrigerator a hunk of Parmesan, for those nights when you haven't had time to get to the shops. That way, within 10 minutes of coming through the door, you can have dinner on the table. No one ever complains that they don't like pasta, even other people's children!

As well as being a great comfort food, a dish of risotto can be a canny way to use up leftover vegetables. Once your rice is right, you can throw anything in for an easy supper. Risotto is a hands-on dish and you'll have to watch it cooking and stir, but done simply it's always a hit. Butternut squash risotto is a favourite of mine – try it!

Even if you've never tried couscous, give it a whirl. I adore it. It miraculously absorbs any sauce that surrounds it, and puffs itself up to a wonderful fluffy cloud. Try my Healthy Couscous (*see* page 118) with a dish of roasted vegetables for a simple vegetarian meal.

Beef & aubergine rigatoni bake with tomato & basil

I found it hard to persuade my children to eat aubergine, so I came up with this dish that breaks it down to silkily mix with two of their favourite things: pasta and minced meat. The key is not to overcook the rigatoni, as it will continue to cook in the oven, so boil it only until slightly firm to the bite (or al dente), then stop cooking immediately and drain.

Serves 4–6
Preparation time 15 minutes
Cooking time 1 hour
Can be made in advance

2 aubergines, cut lengthways into
    1cm (½in) slices
salt flakes and black pepper
300g (10½oz) rigatoni
3 tbsp olive oil, plus extra for the dish
1 onion, finely chopped
1 red chilli, deseeded and finely chopped
2 garlic cloves, finely chopped
500g (1lb 2oz) lean minced beef
3 tbsp tomato purée
2 tbsp Worcestershire sauce
2 × 400g cans chopped tomatoes
handful of basil leaves, finely chopped
600g (1lb 5oz) low-fat cottage cheese,
    drained
100g (3½oz) Parmesan cheese, finely grated
125g (4½oz) ball of mozzarella cheese, sliced

Which pasta shape?

Rigatoni is ideal for this dish, as the thick sauce clings to the ribbed tubes. If you're out of rigatoni, substitute another pasta of a similar shape, such as penne. (In the same way, the tagliatelle I use with my Anchovy, Tomato & Bacon Pasta Sauce – *see* page 107 – can be substituted with similar-shaped linguine or spaghetti.)

1 Put the aubergine slices in a colander, sprinkle generously with salt and stand the colander over a bowl for 15–20 minutes to draw out the water.

2 Bring a large pan of salted water to the boil and cook the pasta for 8–10 minutes, or according to packet instructions, until *al dente*. Drain, drizzle with 1 tbsp of the oil, season and toss. Set aside.

3 Heat another 1 tbsp of the oil in a sauté pan over a medium heat and cook the onion, chilli and garlic for 2–3 minutes, stirring. Add the minced beef and cook for another 5–6 minutes, until it is browned all over. Add the tomato purée and Worcestershire sauce, season, then add the tomatoes and basil. Reduce the heat and simmer for 20 minutes. Preheat the oven to 190°C/375°F/gas mark 5.

4 Meanwhile, rinse the salt from the aubergine slices and pat dry with kitchen paper. Pour the remaining oil into a large nonstick frying pan or griddle placed over a high heat, and fry or griddle the aubergine for 1–2 minutes on each side until golden brown. You may need to do this in batches.

5 Lightly oil a 22 × 28cm (8½ × 11in) deep ovenproof dish. Lay a third of the aubergine into the dish, then spread over half the pasta. Add half the cottage cheese, then half the minced beef and a third of the Parmesan. Repeat the layers, then finish with the remaining aubergine slices and Parmesan. Arrange the mozzarella evenly over the top. Bake for 30 minutes, until bubbling around the sides. Serve hot.

Anchovy, tomato & bacon pasta sauce

This is a great storecupboard recipe. You can substitute dried pasta for the fresh tagliatelle used here, but remember it will double in volume once cooked. This is a little like the Italian puttanesca sauce, though I have omitted the olives – my children find them overpowering – and added bacon. Rinsed capers would go nicely in this as well; use 1 tablespoon if you like them.

Serves 4 hungry children
Preparation time 10 minutes
Cooking time 30 minutes
Can be made in advance to end of step 2

2 tbsp olive oil
1 garlic clove, finely chopped
1 large onion, finely sliced
140g (5oz) bacon or pancetta, sliced
114g can anchovies in olive oil, drained
2 × 400g cans chopped tomatoes
handful of basil leaves, roughly chopped
2 tbsp Worcestershire sauce
salt flakes and black pepper
500g (1lb 2oz) fresh tagliatelle
lots of freshly grated Parmesan cheese

1 Heat half the oil in a large frying pan over a low to medium heat, add the garlic and onion and gently fry, stirring, until softened, then add the bacon or pancetta and fry until golden. Add the anchovies to the frying pan, cooking to allow them to break up slightly.

2 Tip the tomatoes into the pan, add the basil and Worcestershire sauce and season. Stir well and allow to simmer and thicken for at least 25 minutes. The longer you can leave the sauce to simmer, the better. Stir occasionally so it doesn't catch on the bottom of the pan.

3 Bring a large pan of salted water to the boil and cook the pasta according to packet instructions, until *al dente*. Drain, drizzle with the remaining oil, grind over some black pepper and toss.

4 Divide the pasta between 4 warmed serving bowls, and spoon the sauce over. Serve with a generous sprinkle of Parmesan.

Cooking perfect pasta

Use a very large pan filled with boiling water and stir for the first minute of cooking. Always salt the water as this will enhance the flavour of the pasta. If your pan is too small or contains too little water, the pasta will stick and clump together and cook unevenly. Once you add the pasta to the pan, adjust the heat so the water doesn't boil up and spill over the sides. Most dried pasta cooks in about 8–12 minutes, but always test a piece to ensure it is tender though slightly firm to the bite (*al dente*) before draining.

Pasta with bacon & vegetable sauce

To give this dish a simple twist, omit the tomatoes and stir in a couple of spoonfuls of pesto 5 minutes before the sauce is ready (shop-bought pesto is fine!).

Serves 4
Preparation time 15 minutes
Cooking time 30 minutes
Can be made in advance to end of step 1

2 tbsp olive oil
150g (5½oz) fresh breadcrumbs
50g (1¾oz) Parmesan cheese, finely grated
2 tbsp finely chopped basil leaves,
   plus extra to garnish
400g (14oz) spaghetti

For the sauce
1 tbsp olive oil
1 red onion, finely chopped
1 red chilli, deseeded and finely chopped
1 garlic clove, finely chopped
1 courgette, cut into half moons
1 small aubergine, diced
8 rashers of smoked bacon, sliced
400g can tomatoes
12 button mushrooms, halved
small handful of basil leaves
salt flakes and black pepper

1 First make the sauce. Pour the oil into a large saucepan over a medium heat and add the onion, chilli and garlic. Fry gently for 5 minutes, until the onion has softened but not coloured. Add the courgette, aubergine and bacon and cook for 15 minutes, or until the vegetables are tender. Add the tomatoes, mushrooms and basil, taste and season, being generous with the pepper. Simmer for a further 10 minutes.

2 Bring a large pan of salted water to the boil over a high heat, adding ½ tbsp of the oil. Meanwhile, pour 1 tbsp of the oil into a small frying pan over a high heat and toss in the breadcrumbs, stirring constantly until they are toasted a light golden brown. Remove from the heat and mix in the Parmesan and basil. Set aside.

3 Cook the spaghetti in the saucepan of boiling water, following the packet instructions, until *al dente*. Drain, drizzle in the remaining oil, grind over more black pepper and toss.

4 Serve the spaghetti in warmed serving bowls and spoon the sauce over the top, then sprinkle on the toasted breadcrumbs and a little chopped basil.

Pasta: fresh or dried?
Fresh and dried pasta have different roles in the kitchen: generally speaking, dried pasta is firmer when cooked and suits chunkier, oilier, often meaty sauces. It is cheaper and keeps very well. Fresh pasta is better suited to creamy sauces and those with a more delicate flavour.

Simple salmon, dill & crème fraîche pasta

This recipe is so easy. Take care with dill; it is a delicious herb but is also quite strong and you don't want it to overpower the dish. The whole plate should have a delicate tang and be sparkling with subtle flavours.

Serves 4
Preparation time 5–10 minutes
Cooking time 15–20 minutes

4 × 140g (5oz) salmon fillets
salt flakes and black pepper
2 tbsp olive oil
300g (10½oz) spaghetti, preferably fresh
10g (¼oz) dill fronds, finely chopped
finely grated zest and juice of
   1 unwaxed lemon
4–6 tbsp crème fraîche

1 Preheat the oven to 190°C/375°F/gas mark 5.

2 Place the salmon fillets in an ovenproof dish, season and drizzle with half the oil, turning the fillets to coat all sides. Roast in the oven for 10–15 minutes, until the salmon is very moist and still slightly pink in the middle (slice off a chunk to check).

3 Bring a large pan of salted water to the boil over a high heat and cook the pasta according to the packet instructions until *al dente*. Drain, return to the pan and toss with the remaining oil to prevent it from sticking.

4 Meanwhile, flake the salmon into a bowl and toss in the dill and lemon zest. Add to the pasta and gently mix through with the lemon juice and crème fraîche, taking care to keep the fish in large flakes. Season well and serve immediately.

Perfect fish with pasta
When you cook any pasta recipe containing fish, be very sure not to overcook the fish. It needs to remain slightly underdone, as its residual heat combined with the piping hot pasta will continue to cook it when it is added to the sauce. So make sure that it has a faint translucent quality in the centre before you add it to pasta, which indicates that it is slightly undercooked.

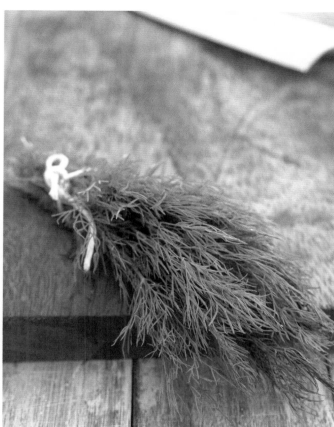

Haddock & spring vegetable risotto

For a slightly healthier version, use half-fat crème fraîche instead of butter. I double-blanch the rice for risottos. You may think this makes it a laborious process, but you'll find that it removes some of the starch and produces a lighter dish as well as cutting down the cooking time.

Serves 4
Preparation time 15 minutes
Cooking time 30 minutes

300g (10½oz) smoked haddock or other
   flaky white fish fillets, undyed, skin on
300ml (½ pint) milk
568ml (1 pint) fish or vegetable stock
2 bay leaves
2 rosemary sprigs
300g (10½oz) risotto rice
1 tbsp olive oil
4 baby courgettes, cut into 1cm (½in) slices
6 asparagus spears, trimmed (*see* secret,
   page 182), cut into 1cm (½in) slices
3 spring onions, finely chopped
10g (¼oz) butter
20g (¾oz) Parmesan cheese, finely grated
finely grated zest and juice of 1 unwaxed lime
small handful of mint leaves, chopped,
   to serve (optional)

1 Lay the haddock in a saucepan and cover with the milk and 250ml (9fl oz) of the stock, adding the bay and rosemary. Place over a medium heat and allow to come to the boil, then turn off the heat and allow the fish to cool in the liquid.

2 Meanwhile, bring a pan of water to the boil over a high heat and add the rice. Boil for 2–3 minutes, then drain. Put the rice back into the rinsed-out saucepan, cover with cold water and bring up to the boil again. Simmer for 3–4 minutes, then pour into a sieve and rinse under cold water to stop it cooking any more.

3 Lift the haddock from the cooking liquid and remove the skin. Strain the cooking liquid and set aside. Flake the haddock, removing as many bones as you can. Set aside.

4 Heat the oil in a large pan, add the risotto rice and stir to coat all the grains. Add a couple of ladles of the reserved haddock liquor, stir and allow it all to be absorbed. Then add a little more, stirring, each time allowing the liquid to be absorbed before adding more, and using as much of the remaining stock as you need. After about 10 minutes of this, add the courgettes and asparagus.

5 Taste the rice; when it's ready it should be *al dente*. Add the spring onions and flaked haddock, gently stir through, then add the butter to thicken the risotto and give it a gloss. Add the Parmesan and keep stirring: you will see the last of the liquid thicken. Add in the lime zest and juice. Serve in warmed bowls and sprinkle each portion with mint.

The wonders of poaching liquor

Never throw away the liquid used for poaching fish. It will contribute to your final dish, making a wonderful stock or sauce. Here it brings fishy, herby flavours to the risotto. For a quick dish, poach a fish fillet, keep it warm while you boil down the poaching liquor to intensify its flavours, then whisk in butter to thicken. A great, speedy sauce!

Chicken, lemon & rocket risotto

Citrus and slightly spicy rocket make this quick, easy dish delicious. Risotto is a hands-on dish – you can't just leave it on the stove – so I tend to make it when the children can sit at the kitchen table at the same time and we go through their spelling homework.

Serves 4 children
Preparation time 10 minutes
Cooking time 45 minutes

1.2 litres (2 pints) good-quality chicken stock
2 skinless chicken breasts
45g (1½oz) unsalted butter
1 red onion, finely chopped
125g (4½oz) risotto rice
100ml (3½fl oz) dry white wine
25g (1oz) rocket leaves
finely grated zest of 1 unwaxed lemon
45g (1½oz) Parmesan cheese, shaved
salt flakes and black pepper

1 Place the chicken stock into a large saucepan, bring to the boil over a high heat, reduce the heat to a simmer and add the chicken breasts. Poach for 10 minutes, then remove a breast to a plate and slice it through. If there is any trace of pink, return the breast to the pan for 2 minutes more, then check it again. Remove the chicken from the pan with a slotted spoon and slice into bite-sized pieces. Keep the stock hot over a low heat.

2 Put 25g (1oz) of the butter in a sauté pan or deep frying pan and melt over a low heat. Add the onion, fry gently until soft, then add the rice and stir gently for 2 minutes. Pour in the wine, allow most of it to be absorbed, then ladle in some of the hot chicken stock and stir until that, too, is absorbed. Continue to add ladles of hot stock to the rice, stirring gently and allowing the stock to be absorbed between each addition, for about 18 minutes, or until the rice is cooked but still *al dente*.

3 Five minutes before the rice is cooked, stir in the chicken slices, rocket, lemon zest, remaining butter and Parmesan. Heat through thoroughly. Taste and adjust the seasoning and serve on warmed plates.

The secret of risotto

You must use short-grained risotto rice when cooking risotto. It has a high starch content, which produces a creamy texture, and the most common types are arborio and carnaroli. Gradually adding hot stock, waiting until each ladle is absorbed before adding the next, and stirring constantly, are the keys to the dish. At the end of cooking, stirring in butter and Parmesan and leaving for 5 minutes before serving will give a creamier finish. Be careful not to overcook the rice as the grains should remain slightly firm to the bite. The overall texture of the finished dish should be gorgeously unctuous and it shouldn't separate into a pile of rice surrounded by a moat of liquid. The Italians have the best phrase for it – *all'onda*, which means the risotto should form 'waves' on the plate if you tip it.

Red rice salad

In my opinion, Camargue red rice is always best used for light salads as it is bulkier than white rice and has a slightly nutty flavour that is complemented by a light dressing. It is really important to have all your ingredients at room temperature: fridge-cold salads are tasteless!

Serves 4
Preparation time 15 minutes
Cooking time 25 minutes
Can be made in advance

200g (7oz) Camargue red rice
2 tbsp olive oil, plus extra to drizzle
1 red chilli, deseeded and finely chopped
20 raw king prawns, peeled and deveined
   (*see* secret, page 92)
salt flakes and black pepper
10 basil leaves, finely sliced
3 spring onions, finely chopped
4 sun-dried tomatoes, thinly sliced
3 tbsp flatleaf parsley, finely chopped

For the dressing
3 tbsp olive oil
1 tbsp grain mustard
finely grated zest and juice of
   1 unwaxed lemon

1 Cook the rice according to the packet instructions. Drain and refresh under cold running water. Drizzle over a little oil to ensure it does not clump together. Set aside.

2 Meanwhile, pour the oil into a frying pan and place over a medium heat until hot. Add the chilli and prawns, season and fry gently for 4–5 minutes until the prawns are cooked through and nicely pink, tossing in the basil towards the end of cooking. Remove from the heat and allow to cool.

3 Pour the rice into a large bowl, stir in the spring onions, sun-dried tomatoes, parsley and cooled prawn mixture. Toss together.

4 Mix together all the ingredients for the dressing and add a pinch each of salt and pepper. Stir the dressing well into the rice salad – be generous with it and allow it to absorb into the rice before serving.

Cooking a perfect pan of rice

Many experienced cooks struggle to make fluffy rice. To achieve it with white rice, weigh out the amount you need, then pour it into a measuring jug. Note the volume, then pour into a pan, adding double the amount of water. Bring to a simmer, cover and cook for 15 minutes, or according to the packet instructions. Remove from the heat, place a clean dish cloth under the lid and set aside for 5 minutes. Fluff up with a fork before serving.

Healthy couscous, my style

This is the perfect accompaniment to meat (it's ideal with my Indian Lamb Chops, see page 46), or simply serve it as a light salad on its own. Couscous has a fabulous ability to soak up any sauce that surrounds it, so it's a great alternative to rice or mashed potatoes.

Serves 6
Preparation time 10–15 minutes

250g (9oz) couscous
olive oil, to drizzle
4 preserved lemons, flesh discarded,
   zest finely chopped
50g (1¾oz) sultanas
50g (1¾oz) toasted flaked almonds
20g (¾oz) mint leaves, finely chopped
20g (¾oz) coriander leaves, finely chopped
salt flakes and black pepper

1 Prepare the couscous (*see* secret, below), adding 300ml (½ pint) boiling water.

2 Simply add all the other ingredients to the couscous, seasoning well, and mix together.

How to prepare couscous
Pour the couscous into a large heatproof bowl and add boiling water, using a ratio of 4 parts couscous to 5 parts boiling water. Add a little oil, fork it through, then cover with clingfilm. Set aside for 5–10 minutes. When the couscous has absorbed the liquid, separate the grains, being careful to remove any clumps with a fork, if necessary adding a little more oil. Cover and set aside for a further 10 minutes.

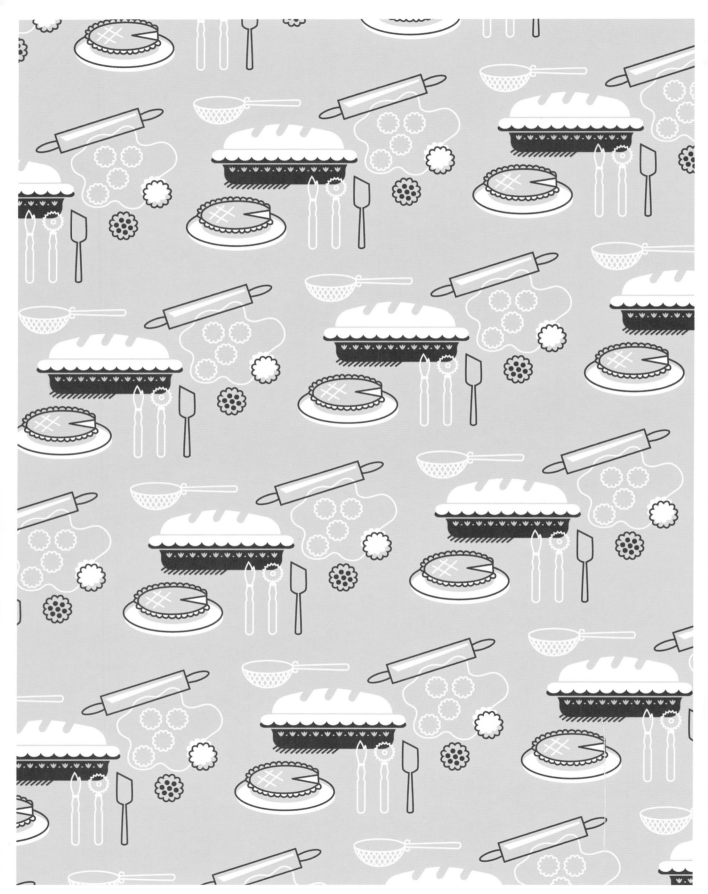

Pies, pastries, tarts & batters

Secrets of cooking pies, pastries, tarts & batters

Pies are a treat in our home, as I don't make them often, but all the family love them. They are a great idea when you have some leftover chicken and bottom-of-the-refrigerator vegetables that have to be eaten.

I have given a recipe for Classic Ham Hock Pie (*see* page 124). We have an amazing butcher and he's very generous with his advice if I want to do something different. He suggested this pie, which is now part of my repertoire as it's deeply comforting, hearty and a bit naughty. It's not for those watching their figure, but I can't think of a better meal for a winter's night.

When we were photographing recipes for this book, I had a perfect moment when we prepared the Impressively Pretty Fruit Tarts (*see* page 138). Just as they were ready, the kids came in from school and all 8 of their eyes were out on stalks! That recipe is best for when you've got a bit of time, but always makes a real impact. I will cook them if my mother-in-law is coming down, to make a good impression! They are great fun to cook and really easy.

In my time, I have bought two deep-fryers and I have always ended up hating them. You can never clean them properly. Now, I deep-fry my Prawn, Chorizo & Baby Courgette Tempura (*see* page 135) in a pan over the stove. Take care, though; you have got to be incredibly wary as oil at that temperature is very unforgiving. Always have your pan on the back of the hob. Send the kids out of the kitchen. Have kitchen paper on the side ready to blot off any excess oil from your fried items. And respect it. Leave the pan to cool down completely and save any old bottles to dispose of the oil.

I love quiche and have no time for those people who say it's old-fashioned. My Ricotta, Pepper & Artichoke Quiche (*see* page 130) is amazing. It is really easy to pull together using ingredients from the refrigerator and storecupboard. If you have vegetarians for lunch (not Gordon's favourite guests!), it's easy to make two quiches, one meat-free – with a salad and my Best-ever Homemade Chips (*see* page 164) if you're feeling naughty – so everyone's happy.

Classic ham hock pie

Puff pastry makes a delicious topping for ham, beef, chicken and even fish pies. It goes very well with creamy – and especially cheesy – sauces. Press the tines of a fork evenly around the edge of the pastry lid both to seal and decorate. This pie is great served with hot new potatoes.

Serves 4–6
Preparation time 30 minutes
Cooking time 3¼ hours
Can be made in advance
Suitable for freezing at end of step 5

1.4kg (3lb 3oz) ham hock
5 garlic cloves, squashed with the
   heel of the hand
5 thyme sprigs
1 leek, halved lengthways
1 onion, quartered
1 carrot, halved lengthways

For the pie
1 swede, cut into 1cm (½in) dice
4 carrots, cut into 1cm (½in) dice
50g (1¾oz) butter
50g (1¾oz) flour, plus extra to dust
3 tbsp double cream
3 tbsp flatleaf parsley, chopped
salt flakes and black pepper
375g (13oz) ready-made puff pastry block
1 free-range egg yolk, beaten

Covering a pie dish
Once you have rolled out the pastry, it's important to seal the pie properly. Choose a dish with a flat rim to it, and brush the rim with either water or egg yolk, then stick on a strip of pastry trimmings. Wrap the pastry loosely around the rolling pin and lay it over the dish. Press it on to the rim with your fingers, crimping or pressing with a fork all the way round.

1 Place the hock in a large pan with the garlic, thyme, leek, onion and carrot. Pour in enough cold water to cover and place over a medium-high heat. Bring to the boil, reduce the heat to a simmer, cover and cook for 2½ hours. It is ready when the meat falls easily from the bone.

2 Towards the end of the cooking time, bring a pan of water to the boil and drop in the swede and carrots for 5 minutes, until they are just slightly underdone. Drain and set aside.

3 When it is cool enough to handle, remove the ham from its stock and pull the meat from the bone in large bite-sized pieces. Discard the bone and skin. Put the ham into a 28 × 18cm (11 × 7in) ovenproof pie dish. Strain the vegetables and herbs from the delicious stock. Preheat the oven to 200°C/400°F/ gas mark 6.

4 Melt the butter over a gentle heat and, when it is bubbling, stir in the flour until it absorbs all the butter and dries out slightly. Gradually whisk in 500ml (18fl oz) of the stock until the sauce thickens, then add the cream and parsley and check the seasoning.

5 Put the swede and carrot into the pie dish and pour over the sauce. Roll out the puff pastry on a floured surface (*see* secret, page 132) and use it to cover the pie dish (*see* secret, left).

6 Brush the top of the pie with egg yolk and bake in the oven for 30 minutes, until golden brown. Serve hot.

Bacon, mushroom & cheese pastry parcels

These turnovers are handy and very portable snacks for a picnic or children's party. They can also be adapted to make canapés or quick lunchtime snacks with the filling of your choice; you can use almost anything in them, but these are the ones my children like best.

Serves 4
Preparation time 10 minutes
Cooking time 30 minutes
Can be made in advance
Suitable for freezing at end of step 3

1 tbsp olive oil, plus extra for the
  baking tray
4 rashers of unsmoked bacon,
  preferably maple, sliced
8 button mushrooms, finely sliced
100g (3½oz) mature Cheddar cheese, grated
4 cherry tomatoes, quartered
2 tbsp chopped basil leaves
salt flakes and black pepper
425g (15oz) ready-rolled puff pastry sheet
1 free-range egg, beaten
plain flour, to dust

1 Preheat the oven to 220°C/425°F/gas mark 7.

2 Heat the oil in a non-stick frying pan over a medium heat and sauté the bacon and mushrooms for 3–4 minutes, or until golden. Remove from the heat, transfer to a large bowl and allow to cool. Add the cheese, tomatoes and basil, season and mix.

3 Cut the pastry sheet into 4 rectangles. Spoon even quantities of the bacon mixture on to half of each rectangle, making sure you leave a 1cm (½in) gap around the edges. Brush these edges with a little of the egg, then fold the other half of the pastry over to encase the filling. With floured fingers, crimp the edges to seal (*see* photographs, pages 128–9). Using a sharp knife, make small slits in the top of each parcel. Brush with the remaining egg.

4 Place on a lightly oiled baking tray and bake for 20–25 minutes until golden brown and the cheese is slightly oozing out of the sides.

5 Serve wrapped in greaseproof paper to cold and hungry kids after football.

How to make a perfect turnover

Be careful not to overfill the pastry or the turnovers might break open, and remember to leave room to crimp and seal the edges. This can be done with a fork or simply with your thumb and finger. Brushing the turnovers with beaten egg before baking helps make them glossy and golden brown.

Ricotta, pepper & artichoke quiche

This is a great way to use up odds and ends from the refrigerator. You can vary the type of cheese you use and the vegetables you put in, according to what you have left over, but this is my favourite, and I always have marinated anchovies and artichokes around.

Serves 4–6
Preparation time 15 minutes,
   plus 1 hour chilling
Cooking time 1 hour
Can be made in advance

90g (3¼oz) marinated peppers,
   sliced into strips
6 marinated artichokes, quartered
10 marinated anchovies
2 free-range eggs, lightly beaten
200g (7oz) ricotta cheese
25g (1oz) Parmesan cheese, grated
90ml (3fl oz) milk
90ml (3fl oz) single cream
salt flakes and black pepper

For the pastry
175g (6oz) plain flour, plus extra to dust
75g (2¾oz) unsalted butter,
   plus extra for the tin

1 First make the pastry. Sift the flour and a pinch of salt into a large bowl. Add the butter, cut into knobs, and rub with your fingertips until the mixture resembles breadcrumbs. Add enough cold water to bring together to a firm dough, then wrap in clingfilm and rest it in the refrigerator for 30 minutes.

2 Roll out the pastry on a floured surface and use it to line a well-buttered 22cm (8½in) flan tin. Chill for a further 30 minutes in the refrigerator.

3 Preheat the oven to 190°C/375°F/gas mark 5.

4 Remove the pastry case from the fridge and blind bake for 20 minutes (*see* secret, page 142). Remove the beans and greaseproof paper and return to the oven for another 5 minutes. Set aside to cool and reduce the oven temperature to 170°C/340°F/gas mark 3.

5 Layer the peppers, artichokes and anchovies in the pastry case. Whisk together all the other filling ingredients and ladle the mixture in; it should just reach the top of the pastry case. Bake for 35–40 minutes until ready (*see* secret, below).

6 Remove the quiche from the oven and allow to rest for 10–15 minutes, then slice and serve.

A perfectly cooked quiche
Quiche should have a velvety, slightly wobbly filling, not one of hard-set rubberiness. To achieve this silky texture, make sure you do not overcook it. It is ready when the top is beginning to become golden brown and the middle of the quiche has a wobble to it when you shake the flan tin. If the centre feels springy to the touch, I'm afraid you've gone too far!

Pissaladière

This is my variation on the tart I have enjoyed in the south of France. There are many arguments about what's in the classic dish – whether it has tomatoes or not, and which pastry to use – but this is the version I enjoy the most and love to eat hot or cold. If you're not keen on olives, use 1 tablespoon rinsed capers instead.

Serves 4
Preparation time 30 minutes
Cooking time 40 minutes
Can be made in advance

375g (13oz) ready-rolled puff pastry block
plain flour, to dust
4 tbsp olive oil, plus extra for the
   baking sheet
1 free-range egg yolk
1 large onion, finely sliced
2 garlic cloves, crushed
4 plum tomatoes, roughly chopped
2 tbsp tomato purée
1 tsp fresh thyme leaves
black pepper
2 × 50g cans anchovy fillets, drained
70g (2½oz) black olives, stoned

1 Preheat the oven to 200°C/400°F/gas mark 6.

2 Roll out the pastry on a floured surface into a rectangle measuring about 30 × 24cm (12 × 9½in) and ½cm (¼in) thick. Place on a lightly oiled baking sheet and, using a sharp knife, score a border about 2cm (¾in) from the edge all the way around. Brush this edge with egg yolk to help make it beautifully golden brown when cooked.

3 Heat half the oil in a large frying pan over a gentle heat and sauté the onion and garlic very slowly. They need to become very soft but not brown. Add the tomatoes and cook for 10 minutes, or until the liquid has virtually evaporated. Add the tomato purée, thyme and pepper, stir and cook for a further 4–5 minutes. Remove from the heat and allow to cool slightly.

4 Transfer the onion and tomato mixture on to the pastry and arrange the anchovy fillets on top in a lattice formation, then arrange the olives on top and drizzle over the remaining oil. Place in the oven for 20–25 minutes, or until the pastry is puffed around the edges and golden brown.

5 Allow to cool slightly before serving, or serve at room temperature.

Rolling out pastry

It is important to have a cool work surface – away from the hob if possible – and to dust both the surface and your rolling pin with flour to stop the pastry from sticking. Take the pastry from the fridge and allow it to lose a little of its chill before rolling; if it is too cold it may crack. Apply gentle pressure with the rolling pin, turning the pastry occasionally for an even thickness and to prevent it from sticking to the work surface, dusting with a little more flour if needed. When using puff pastry, never re-roll trimmings as they won't rise.

Breakfast rolls

Ring the changes to these delicious rolls by using merguez instead of plain pork sausages, or even adding a spoonful of curry paste. They are wonderful to have on standby in the freezer, to pull out for an emergency brunch, to reinvigorate Sunday footballers or just for those mornings when you're feeling a little fragile after a late night!

Serves 4
Preparation time 5–10 minutes
Cooking time 35–40 minutes
Can be made in advance
Suitable for freezing at end of step 2

4 large pork sausages
10 pancetta slices
375g (13oz) ready-rolled puff pastry sheet,
    cut into 4 squares
1 free-range egg, beaten
2 tbsp tomato purée
2 tbsp grated Parmesan cheese
salt flakes

1 Tightly wrap 2 of the pork sausages in 5 slices of pancetta each. Lightly brush the edge of each pastry square with a little of the egg. Wrap each of the pancetta-wrapped sausages in a square of puff pastry, allowing the ends to poke out.

2 Spread 1 tbsp tomato purée on the remaining pastry squares, sprinkle with the Parmesan, place on a sausage and roll tightly; gently fold over the ends on these rolls to encase the cheese and tomato filling.

3 Brush each roll with beaten egg, transfer to a baking sheet lined with greaseproof paper and refrigerate for 20 minutes to rest the pastry. Meanwhile, preheat the oven to 180°C/350°F/gas mark 4. Sprinkle the rolls with salt, then bake for 35–40 minutes, until golden brown.

4 Remove the rolls from the oven and allow to cool for 10–15 minutes before serving.

Pretty pastries

There are several things you can do to make these or any other pastries look really professional. Always finish with a glaze. Milk will do for ease and economy, but beaten egg will make them beautifully golden, while beaten egg yolk gives extra glossiness. Try sprinkling with poppy or sesame seeds before baking, but always check that your guests are not allergic to sesame before serving.

Prawn, chorizo &
baby courgette tempura

Make sure you get raw chorizo for this recipe; cooked chorizo is not suitable for deep-frying as it will become very tough indeed. These are great as a starter or a party nibble with my Chilli & Lime Mayonnaise (see page 274).

Serves 4
Preparation time 5–10 minutes
Cooking time 10 minutes
Can be made in advance

vegetable oil, to deep-fry
plain flour, to coat
360g (12½oz) raw tiger prawns, peeled
    and deveined (*see* secret, page 92)
4 raw chorizo sausages, cut into even chunks
200g (7oz) baby courgettes, sliced lengthways
lime wedges, to serve

For the batter
85g (3oz) plain flour
1 tbsp cornflour
½ tsp salt
200ml (7fl oz) ice-cold sparkling
    mineral water
2 ice cubes

1 Pour enough oil into a deep saucepan to make a layer 5cm (2in) deep. Place over a medium heat until the temperature on a cook's thermometer reads 180°C/356°F. If you don't have a cook's thermometer, the oil is hot enough when a cube of bread will sizzle and turn brown when dropped in.

2 To make the batter, place the flour, cornflour and salt into a large mixing bowl. Whisk in the water; do not over-mix but make sure it is all combined. Add the ice cubes to keep it really cold.

3 Place the plain flour on a plate and use it to dredge the prawns, chorizo and courgettes, shaking off any excess. Dip the items into the batter, then carefully add each to the hot oil, standing well back. Deep-fry in batches for 2–3 minutes (*see* secret, below) or until crisp and golden. Carefully remove with a slotted spoon and keep warm while you cook the rest.

4 Serve with lime wedges to squeeze over.

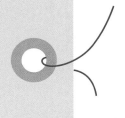

How to deep-fry
You have to take great care when deep-frying to avoid burns and kitchen fires. Never leave the pan of hot oil unattended, and never fill a pan more than half full. Add your items in batches, taking care not to overcrowd the pan or they will emerge soggy rather than crisp. Using a slotted spoon, turn the items once or twice so all sides brown evenly, then remove and blot excess oil on kitchen paper.

Impressively pretty fruit tarts

Presentation is key here. I have mentioned raspberries in the recipe, but you can choose blackberries, blueberries or strawberries depending on the season. I find these work best as individual tarts; you will need nine 10cm (4in) tart tins.

Makes nine 10cm (4in) tarts
Preparation time 10 minutes,
  plus 2 hours cooling
Cooking time 17 minutes
Can be made in advance to end of step 2

500g (1lb 2oz) sweet shortcrust pastry
  (*see* page 142)
600g (1lb 5oz) pastry cream (*see* page 141)
400g (14oz) fresh raspberries
3 tbsp raspberry jam (optional)
2 tbsp icing sugar (optional)

Avoid a soggy base
To keep your tart bases crisp and toothsome, bake the pastry cases as described above (first filled with baking beans, then without) to seal them and give a biscuit bite. Fill with the pastry cream only just before serving to minimise the risk of any soaking into the case.

1 Preheat the oven to 180°C/350°F/gas mark 4.

2 Roll out the pastry, use it to line the tart tins and blind bake (*see* page 142) for 12 minutes. Remove the beans and papers then return to the oven for a further 5 minutes. Leave to cool for at least 2 hours.

3 Divide the pastry cream between the pastry cases and smooth the tops.

4 Cut the raspberries in half lengthways and arrange over the pastry cream, starting from the edge and moving into the centre in a circle formation.

5 Spoon the jam (if liked) into a small pan, add 1 tbsp water and place over a low heat until it melts, then push through a sieve. Gently brush this glaze on the raspberries.

6 Alternatively, put the icing sugar (if liked) in a tea strainer and shake it evenly over the tarts.

Remarkably easy pastry cream

I was really worried the first time I tried this as, before, I had followed recipes that sent me into complete meltdown. But here is my easy solution; I have yet to mess it up! It's great for éclairs and tart fillings. Substitute 1 teaspoon vanilla extract if you don't have vanilla pods.

Makes 600g (1lb 5oz) – enough to fill
a 24cm (9½in) pastry case
Preparation time 5 minutes,
plus 3 hours chilling
Cooking time 15 minutes
Can be made in advance

475ml (17fl oz) milk
100g (3½oz) caster sugar
1 vanilla pod (optional)
5 free-range egg yolks
30g (1oz) plain flour
55g (2oz) unsalted butter

Cooking perfect pastry cream

Make sure you don't cook the cream over a high heat as it may catch at the bottom of the pan. Use a spatula and whisk, taking care to reach all the corners, and stir continuously. Be patient and, once it has thickened, strain it through a sieve. Remember it will continue to thicken while cooling. Laying a sheet of clingfilm directly on the surface will prevent a skin from forming and leave you with lovely, silky-smooth cream – delicious!

1 Pour the milk and half the sugar into a saucepan. Slice the vanilla pod (if liked) lengthways and add it to the pan. Place over a medium heat and bring to the boil, then remove from the heat.

2 Place the egg yolks and remaining sugar in a large mixing bowl and, using a handheld electric whisk, beat briskly until pale in colour. Add the flour, continuing to whisk.

3 Remove the vanilla pod (if using) from the hot milk, scrape out the black, sticky seeds with the point of a knife and return these to the milk. Discard the empty pod. Very slowly pour half the milk into the egg-flour mixture, whisking constantly, then pour this back into the saucepan and place it over a low to medium heat. Pour in the rest of the milk, still whisking all the time.

4 From now on, I alternate between a spatula to scrape the bottom and sides of the pan to make sure none of the mix is sticking, and a whisk to whisk the cream. You will see the pastry cream thickening. Allow it to come to the boil, still stirring and whisking constantly, for no more than 1 minute, then remove from the heat and pour through a sieve into a cold mixing bowl. Add the butter and stir gently until melted.

5 Lay a piece of clingfilm on the surface of the pastry cream to stop a skin from forming. Set aside to cool a little, then place it in the refrigerator to chill for at least 3 hours. Now you are ready to use your homemade pastry cream – and you should be proud!

Homemade sweet shortcrust pastry

I used to buy ready-made shortcrust pastry until one day I forgot. Reluctantly, I had a go at making my own. I've never bought a packet since. Use a food mixer and dough hook to stop your hands making the dough too warm; otherwise, run your hands under cold water to cool them.

Makes about 500g (1lb 2oz) or enough
   for two 25cm (10in) tarts
Preparation time 15 minutes,
   plus 45 minutes chilling
Cooking time 25 minutes
Can be made in advance
Suitable for freezing

250g (9oz) plain flour, plus extra to dust
50g (1¾oz) icing sugar
125g (4½oz) cold unsalted butter,
   cut into cubes, plus extra for the tin
2 large free-range eggs
dash of milk

Preparing a pastry case

Follow the instructions for rolling out pastry on page 132. Loosely wrap the pastry around the rolling pin, then unroll it over a lightly buttered tart tin. Do not stretch the pastry over the tin as this will cause it to shrink during baking. Gently press the pastry into the edges of the tin and trim off the excess. Use the trimmings to patch any holes in the case. Prick the pastry base all over with a fork to ensure there are no air bubbles, then chill to prevent any shrinkage in the oven. Line the tin with greaseproof paper and fill with baking beans or raw rice to prevent the base from rising.

1 Sift the flour and icing sugar into a large mixing bowl and add the butter cubes. Using your fingertips, rub the butter in until the mixture resembles fine breadcrumbs. At this stage, either continue with your hands or transfer to a food mixer with a dough hook.

2 Beat together 1 of the eggs with the milk, add this to the flour mixture and mix until it just comes together into a crumbly ball of dough. Do not overwork it: it should look a little dry. Add a little more flour if needed.

3 Shape the dough into a ball, wrap it in clingfilm and refrigerate for at least 45 minutes or up to a day.

4 It is often necessary to 'blind bake' the pastry. To do this, remove the clingfilm and roll the pastry out on a floured surface, using a floured rolling pin, until 5mm (¼in) thick. Use it to line a lightly buttered tart tin (*see* secret, left). Cover with clingfilm and return to the refrigerator for 30 minutes. Preheat the oven to 180°C/350°F/gas mark 4.

5 Line the pastry with greaseproof paper and fill with baking beans or raw rice, to prevent the pastry rising. Bake in the oven for 20 minutes, until golden brown. Remove the greaseproof paper and baking beans or rice. Beat the remaining egg, use it to brush the pastry all over, then return to the oven for another 5 minutes to seal the pastry; this stops the base becoming soggy. Remove from the oven and allow to cool before filling.

Traditional treacle tart

This is the kind of pudding I love, but I keep it for special occasions! It needs a little forward-planning as the filling is best made the day before and the pastry needs time in the refrigerator. But, after that's done, it is an easy pudding to put together on a busy entertaining day. This is delicious served with a large dollop of crème fraîche.

Serves 8
Preparation time 15 minutes,
  plus overnight chilling
Cooking time 45 minutes
Can be made in advance to end of step 2

55g (2oz) ground almonds
finely grated zest of 1 unwaxed orange
85g (3oz) fresh white breadcrumbs
340g (12oz) golden syrup
125ml (4½fl oz) double cream
1 large free-range egg
butter for the tin
350g (12oz) sweet shortcrust pastry
  (*see* opposite)

1 Mix the almonds, orange zest and breadcrumbs in a large bowl. Spoon the golden syrup into a small pan, warm over a low heat until runny, then add to the breadcrumbs and stir well. Beat together the cream and egg and gradually fold them into the syrup mix. Cover the bowl with clingfilm and refrigerate overnight.

2 Lightly butter a loose-bottomed, fluted 24cm (9½in) tart tin, roll out the shortcrust pastry until 5mm (¼in) thick (*see* secret, page 132) and line the tin (*see* secret, page 142). Cover with clingfilm and refrigerate for at least 20 minutes.

3 Preheat the oven to 150°C/300°F/gas mark 2.

4 Transfer the filling into the tart case and bake in the oven for 45–50 minutes, until golden brown and just set.

Making breadcrumbs

Simply remove the crusts from day-old bread, roughly chop, throw them in the food processor, then blitz. Seal the crumbs in a polythene food bag and freeze. Add to them whenever you have stale bread until you have enough to make yourself a treat – like the recipe above – for all your hard work! Bought breadcrumbs are relatively expensive and often have colourings and other nasties in them that we can all do without.

Pineapple tart tatin

This has to be one of the prettiest puddings there is and it looks much more impressive and complicated than it actually is to make! It is especially delicious when served with a scoop of my Coconut Sorbet (see page 214). You'll need four 10cm (4in) tart tins.

Serves 4
Preparation time 10 minutes, plus
   30 minutes cooling/chilling
Cooking time 20 minutes
Can be made in advance to end of step 3

4 × 2cm (¾in) thick slices of ripe pineapple
50g (1¾oz) caster sugar
knob of butter
dash of coconut-flavoured liqueur
375g (13oz) ready-rolled puff pastry sheet

Making caramel
Don't be scared of making caramel, but do take care, as sugar burns are very nasty. Melt the sugar in a clean pan, swirling it occasionally to get an even colour (but never stirring). Make sure that every single grain of sugar has melted. Watch it like a hawk as there's a world of difference between caramel and burned sugar! If it starts to burn, immediately plunge the pan's base into cold water to stop the cooking process.

1 Remove and discard the hard central core from each pineapple slice. Place a frying pan over a medium heat and add the sugar (*see* secret, below). Watching constantly, wait until it turns a good caramel colour, then add the butter and allow it to melt and bubble. Add a glug of liqueur – watch your eyebrows; it will flame up! Let this mixture bubble together, then divide it between the 4 tart tins and refrigerate it for 10 minutes to cool and firm up.

2 Place a pineapple ring on the top of each caramel base and push it down slightly.

3 Cut out 4 rounds of pastry, each slightly bigger than the tart tins. Drape over the top of the pineapple, then tuck in the edges well to encase the pineapple completely. Refrigerate for up to 20 minutes to prevent the pastry from shrinking in the oven.

4 Preheat the oven to 200°C/400°F/gas mark 6.

5 Bake for 20–25 minutes, until the tarts are cooked and golden.

6 Remove from the oven and rest for 10 minutes, then very carefully slide a knife around the sides of each tart to loosen. Place a serving plate on top of each, then flip it over to invert the tart tatins. Do this very carefully as caramel can burn!

Fresh cherry jam tart

This is a quick pudding that the kids will love. Replace the cherries with strawberries, raspberries or blueberries when they're in season if you wish. Just make sure, whichever fruit you use, that it isn't over-ripe, as it needs to hold its shape once cooked.

Serves 4
Preparation time 15 minutes
Cooking time 20 minutes
Can be made in advance to end of step 3

375g (13oz) ready-rolled puff pastry sheet,
　cut in half
500g (1lb 2oz) fresh cherries,
　stoned and halved
2 tsp icing sugar
100ml (3½fl oz) Pimm's
1 tsp cornflour
1 free-range egg, beaten
1 tbsp golden caster sugar

1 Place the pastry squares on a baking sheet lined with greaseproof paper. Score a square rim 2.5cm (1in) from the edge of each (*see* secret, below) and then refrigerate for 20–30 minutes.

2 Meanwhile, preheat the oven to 200°C/400°F/gas mark 6 and prepare the tart filling. Place a saucepan over a medium heat and, when it is hot, toss in the cherries and icing sugar. Stir, then add the Pimm's. Watch out for the flame! Allow the mixture to thicken and bubble.

3 Mix the cornflour in a small bowl with 2 tsp cold water to make a paste (this is known as 'slaking' cornflour) and stir it in with the cherries. When the mixture is syrupy, transfer it to a large plate and allow it to cool completely.

4 Spoon the cherries into the centre of each scored square on the pastry, leaving 2.5cm (1in) clear around the sides. Brush the pastry rim with egg and sprinkle with the golden caster sugar.

5 Bake the tarts in the oven for 15–20 minutes, until the pastry is nicely golden. Allow to cool before serving. Each square will serve 2.

Making a puff pastry rim

It is easy and quick to make sweet or savoury tarts with ready-rolled puff pastry, but you will have to create a rim to enclose the filling. To do this, score the pastry (make sure you do not cut all the way through it) with a butter knife. This enables the layers of pastry to puff up while baking. If you neglect to do this, you will have an untidy, perhaps leaking, tart.

Filo lemon tart

I particularly like this with lemon marmalade, but you can, of course, use any flavour of jam you like. Filo pastry, found in the freezer section of most supermarkets, is lighter than shortcrust pastry, and gives an amazing brittle crust that shatters at the touch of a knife.

Makes 12 slices
Preparation time 15 minutes
Cooking time 20 minutes

8 ready-prepared filo pastry sheets
  (*see* secret, below)
50g (1¾oz) butter, melted
150g (5½oz) lemon marmalade
20g (¾oz) sunflower seeds
1 tbsp caster sugar

1 Preheat the oven to 200°C/400°F/gas mark 6.

2 Find a baking sheet that's about the same size as the filo sheets. Brush some butter over the baking sheet, then lay on 4 sheets of filo, one by one, buttering between each (*see* secret, below).

3 Place the marmalade in a small bowl and give it a vigorous stir to loosen it up. Spoon it over the filo pastry, being generous, then sprinkle with half the sunflower seeds. Repeat the layering with the remaining filo pastry, ending with the top layer buttered, then sprinkle with the remaining sunflower seeds and the sugar.

4 Bake the tart for 20 minutes, until it is golden and crispy at the edges. Remove from the oven, allow to cool for 5 minutes, then cut into slices.

Working with filo pastry

Filo pastry is delicious, but quick to dry out. Because of this, you must ensure it is always covered when you work with it; use a slightly dampened, clean dish cloth. Every sheet must be brushed with butter before baking, as otherwise the pastry will be dry and tasteless rather than crispy and delicious. Melt some butter and spread it over the pastry sheet, making sure you cover the entire surface.

Vegetables

Stuffed marrow · Cauliflower cheese my way · Filled potato skins

Tarka dal · Best-ever homemade chips · Rosemary roast parsnips

Honey & thyme roast swede · Roast beetroot with crème fraîche & chives

Green beans with lemon & pancetta · Cream cheese broad beans & garden peas

Mangetout salad · Curly kale with anchovies, onion & garlic

Pan-fried corn on the cob · Stuffed mushrooms · Asparagus soup · Celery soup

Fresh green salad with bacon · Chinese leaf & chilli salad

New potato salad with crème fraîche & coriander

Secrets of cooking vegetables

The most important thing to remember is to shop seasonally and buy locally. Read the labels to see where vegetables are from, and shop by sight and smell. Choose what looks best in the shop rather than being led by a recipe. And remember, you can always smell the best tomatoes.

When selecting salad, think what you'll serve it with and go for the colours and textures of leaves that will best complement the rest of your meal. Choose crispy Iceberg lettuce to use as a wrap or to give some crunch with my Filled Potato Skins (*see* page 160), or buy softer Little Gems to serve with a prawn cocktail.

Use your head and save your pennies. There is no need to buy ready-trimmed vegetables. You will pay a premium and, really, how long will it take to do them yourself? There are other benefits, too: carrots look beautiful when still adorned with their greenery and children love to see them.

Don't attempt to do your vegetable shopping for the whole week in one go. Of course, you can make sure you have root vegetables in, such as potatoes and carrots, but, if you can, pick up a few fresh, lively greens every couple of days.

Check your local independent butcher – they often carry more unusual varieties of seasonal vegetables.

Don't just boil vegetables. It may put your children off – mine certainly went through a phase of calling boiled courgettes slimy cucumbers! But once I began to use my imagination and blanched them, then pan-fried them with garlic, lemon zest and Parmesan until crisp on the outside, they became a favourite.

I am a true believer in steamed vegetables. Gordon thinks it takes too long, but he's wrong! This method retains so much goodness. And you will only need one steamer stack on the hob, rather than millions of different pans.

When you are faced with a marathon meal to prepare, such as Christmas lunch or a large family roast, par-boil your vegetables before the chaos begins. That way, you will be ahead of the game as they will need only a brief second cook before serving.

Never overlook squashes. Butternut squash, especially, is so adaptable. Simply roast it, skin on, with garlic and rosemary, or even dice and mash it. It is the perfect partner to fish or chicken dishes and, when mixed with gravy, it's delicious.

Stuffed marrow

My mum used to make these, but she stuffed the marrow with minced meat and grated Cheddar cheese over the top. This is great comfort food, and a good way to introduce children to marrow. For a larger meal, serve two marrow rings per person on a bed of rice.

Serves 6 as a starter
Preparation time 10 minutes
Cooking time 35 minutes
Can be made in advance to end of step 3

1 medium marrow, sliced into 2.5cm (1in)
   rings and deseeded (*see* secret, below)
3 tbsp olive oil
salt flakes and black pepper

For the stuffing
1 tbsp olive oil
1 garlic clove, crushed
1 thyme sprig
5 baby courgettes, sliced into
   5mm (¼in) thick slices
8 baby plum tomatoes, quartered
40g (1½oz) breadcrumbs
50g (1¾oz) Parmesan cheese, finely grated
25g (1oz) almonds, chopped

1 Preheat the oven to 180°C/350°F/gas mark 4.

2 Place the marrow rings in an ovenproof dish so they fit snugly. Drizzle with the oil and season. Cook in the oven for 20 minutes, or until golden and quite soft. Keep the oven on.

3 Meanwhile, make the stuffing. Pour the oil into a pan and place over a medium heat. Add the garlic and thyme and fry gently for 1–2 minutes, then add the courgettes and stir until they take on a light colour. Toss in the tomatoes and sauté for a couple of minutes to break them down a little.

4 Sprinkle half the breadcrumbs into the hole in each marrow ring to soak up any moisture, then divide the courgette mix between the rings. Sprinkle over the remaining breadcrumbs, the Parmesan and almonds, grind over black pepper and cook in the oven for 15 minutes, or until golden.

The much-neglected marrow

Marrow, a member of the squash family, is extremely versatile and can be sautéed, baked, steamed or fried. The flavour of marrow is similar to courgette and it will go a long way, so it is an inexpensive choice. Pick a firm, small to medium marrow with shiny green skin for the best flavour. When preparing a marrow, top and tail it and remove the seeds from the middle with a spoon.

Cauliflower cheese my way

This is a rich and comforting dish. I hated bland cauliflower cheese with overcooked cauliflower at school, but here is a great, light alternative. However, for those who want the more traditional recipe, I have given a method for cheese sauce here as well (see secret, below).

Serves 4 as a side dish
Preparation time 10–15 minutes
Cooking time 25 minutes
Can be made in advance to end of step 3

1 cauliflower
salt flakes and black pepper
250ml (9fl oz) crème fraîche
2 free-range egg yolks
10g (¼oz) Parmesan cheese, finely grated
100g (3½oz) Dolcelatte cheese
3–4 tbsp breadcrumbs
pinch of cayenne pepper

1 Preheat the oven to 200°C/400°F/gas mark 6.

2 Separate the cauliflower into quite large florets. Bring a pan of salted water to the boil over a high heat, add the florets and cook for 5–10 minutes until tender (the time it takes will depend on their size). You should be able to pierce a floret without any resistance using a sharp knife. Drain and set aside.

3 Find an ovenproof dish that fits all the florets in snugly, place them in and put in the oven for 5 minutes to dry a little. Remove and drain very well again, then return to the dish.

4 To make the sauce, mix together the crème fraîche, egg yolks and Parmesan. Season well and stir. Pour the sauce over the cauliflower, then crumble over the Dolcelatte, in large pieces, and sprinkle on the breadcrumbs and cayenne pepper.

5 Cook in the oven for 15–20 minutes until golden and bubbling.

How to make a cheese sauce

Traditionally this dish has a cheese sauce and it's useful to know how to make it. Simply melt 40g (1½oz) butter in a pan over a gentle heat and stir in 3 tbsp plain flour. Stir for 3–4 minutes to cook out the raw flour taste, then whisk in 300ml (½ pint) hot milk, little by little, stirring constantly to avoid lumps. Bubble for 5 minutes, until thickened, then flavour with grated cheese.

Filled potato skins

I love these. The kids first had them in a local restaurant and I've been trying to perfect my version ever since. I see it as a challenge, as children will always tell you the truth when you ask them for their opinion of a dish!

Serves 4
Preparation time 10 minutes
Cooking time 45 minutes
Can be made in advance

4 large baking potatoes, unpeeled
olive oil, to drizzle, plus extra for
   the baking sheet
salt flakes and black pepper
4 large free-range eggs
3 tbsp half-fat crème fraîche
1 small punnet mustard cress, cut
1 tsp cayenne pepper (optional)

1 Preheat the oven to 220°C/425°F/gas mark 7.

2 Wash and dry the potatoes and prepare and prick the skins (*see* secret, below). Pop them each in a microwave on full power for 13 minutes, or until fully cooked, turning halfway through the cooking time. The potatoes will stay plump instead of shrinking as they can do in the oven.

3 Remove the potatoes, halve lengthways and remove the soft inner flesh to a bowl, leaving only about ½cm (¼in) as a shell. Oil a baking sheet, lay in the potato skins, drizzle with more oil and sprinkle with salt. Bake for 15–20 minutes, until really nice and crispy.

4 Meanwhile, bring a pan of water to the boil and cook the eggs for 5–6 minutes; they should be very slightly soft in the middle. Peel and mash until chunky, then season. Add the crème fraîche and reserved potato flesh and gently mix through. Reduce the oven temperature to 180°C/350°F/gas mark 4. Divide the filling between the crispy potato skins and bake for 10 minutes, until piping hot.

5 Remove from the oven and arrange on a serving plate. Sprinkle with the cress and a little cayenne pepper, if liked.

The best baked potatoes

Choose floury potatoes with a dry texture, such as Maris Piper or King Edward: once baked, they turn beautifully light and fluffy. To make the skins crisp, either wet the potatoes or rub some oil into the skins and roll in sea salt before baking. Always prick the potatoes with a small knife or fork before cooking, especially if you are using a microwave, otherwise you may have a small explosion!

Tarka dal

You will need a saucepan with a lid for this recipe but, if in dire need, use foil instead. Wrap a double layer tightly around the pot, sealing around the sides so steam can't escape. If the foil is not airtight, the dish will lose moisture and may burn.

Serves 4 as a side dish
Preparation time 10 minutes
Cooking time 30 minutes
Can be made in advance

200g (7oz) split red lentils
2 tsp salt flakes
25g (1oz) unsalted butter
1 red onion, finely chopped
2 garlic cloves, crushed
1 tsp ground turmeric
2 tsp garam masala
10g (¼oz) coriander leaves, finely chopped

1 Pour the lentils into a sieve and place under running water to rinse. Transfer them to a saucepan, adding 800ml (1⅓ pints) cold water, then place over a medium heat and bring to the boil. Reduce the heat to a gentle simmer for 10 minutes, skimming any scum off the top, then partly cover with the lid and leave to bubble gently for 20 minutes. You should end up with a thickened yellow soup. Check that the lentils are ready (*see* secret, below), then add the salt.

2 Meanwhile, gently melt the butter in a frying pan and add the onion and garlic, stirring for 5–10 minutes, or until they soften. Add the turmeric and garam masala and mix well. Give the lentils a good stir, then add the onions to them and stir through.

3 Check the seasoning and stir in the chopped coriander, reserving 1 tsp to sprinkle over the top when serving.

How to cook lentils

These pulses are a terrific storecupboard ingredient as they don't need to be soaked before cooking, unlike dried beans and chickpeas. Always rinse lentils before use, as they can be dusty, and place them in a large pan to let them expand as they cook. When ready they should retain their shape but be tender within – taste to check.

Best-ever homemade chips

I love chips and these are delicious and go with everything. They certainly make a virtuous salad seem like more of a meal! I'm a firm believer in having everything in moderation... but these chips are hard to moderate because they are so good!

Serves 4–6
Preparation time 5 minutes
Cooking time 10 minutes

vegetable oil, for deep-frying
8 Maris Piper potatoes, sliced into
   even-sized chips
salt flakes

1 Heat the oil in a deep-fryer to 130°C/266°F.

2 Place the chips into the fryer and cook for 5 minutes, until slightly softened but without any colour. Remove, drain well and blot on kitchen paper to remove any excess oil, then allow to cool completely.

3 Turn the fryer temperature up to 185°C/365°F. Return the chips to the fryer and cook them for 3–4 minutes, or until golden and crispy. Remove from the oil, drain well and blot again on kitchen paper. Sprinkle over the salt while the chips are piping hot and serve immediately.

Choosing potatoes for chips

The best chips come from the most suitable potatoes, so select Maris Piper, King Edward or Desirée varieties. I use Maris Pipers here; they have a pleasant floury texture that is ideal not only for chips but also for roast potatoes, mash and wedges.

Rosemary roast parsnips

These are especially lovely with roast chicken. The cumin gives them a pungent depth that offsets the sweetness of the parsnips brilliantly, while the rosemary lends them a strong herbal fragrance. Don't be tempted to use more rosemary than suggested here as it can be overpowering.

Serves 4 as a side dish
Preparation time 5 minutes
Cooking time 25–30 minutes

2 tbsp olive oil, plus extra for the tray
6 parsnips, halved and cored
12 rosemary sprigs
1 tsp ground cumin
salt flakes and black pepper

1 Preheat the oven to 200°C/400°F/gas mark 6.

2 Line an oven tray that will fit all the parsnips in a single layer with greaseproof paper, then add the parsnips, rosemary, oil and cumin. Season very well and toss so that all the parsnips are well covered with their seasonings.

3 Cook in the oven for 25–30 minutes, or until the parsnips are slightly golden and crisp and wonderfully tender within.

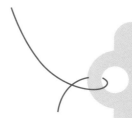

Roasting with herbs

Herbs add a wonderful flavour dimension to any roasted dish, whether it's meat, fish or vegetables. But make sure you use only robust, twiggy herbs for roasting, such as the rosemary here, thyme or bay; their essential oils will survive the cooking process. Delicate herbs with soft leaves such as parsley, dill or tarragon will not stand up well to the intense heat, and will simply shrivel and lose their aroma.

Honey & thyme roast swede

Swede is a great-value vegetable. However, it can be bitter, which is often offputting to children. In this recipe, the sweetness of the honey corrects any such tendency. You'll find this makes a popular side dish for everyone at the table.

Serves 4 as a side dish
Preparation time 5–10 minutes
Cooking time 40 minutes
Can be made in advance
Suitable for freezing

1 large swede, evenly diced
salt flakes and black pepper
2 tbsp olive oil
6 thyme sprigs
2 tbsp runny honey
1 tbsp balsamic vinegar

1 Preheat the oven to 180°C/350°F/gas mark 4.

2 Place the swede in a pan of cold salted water, bring to the boil over a high heat and cook for 8–10 minutes. Drain well, transfer to a large nonstick roasting tin and pop into the oven for 5 minutes to dry out. Remove, add the oil and thyme, season and toss to coat.

3 Drizzle over the honey and balsamic vinegar and roast for 25 minutes, stirring occasionally, until golden and slightly crisp at the edges (*see* secret, below).

Cooking with honey

Nonstick roasting dishes and baking sheets are your friends when using honey in the oven. Though it will add a wonderful sweetness and give a beautiful burnished colour, it is worryingly easy to burn, turning black, acrid in flavour and impossible to chip off traditional baking ware. Keep a close eye on the dish in the oven, basting and stirring frequently and watching out for any scorching.

Roast beetroot with crème fraîche & chives

Delicious, fresh beetroot is enjoying a revival as people are discovering that there are so many ways to prepare this versatile vegetable – and we're not talking about pickling! One taste of these roast beetroots and you'll be a convert!

Serves 4 as a side dish
Preparation time 5 minutes
Cooking time 1 hour

4 raw beetroot, with leaves
4 tbsp olive oil
salt flakes and black pepper

To serve
4 tbsp crème fraîche
4 tsp snipped chives

1 Preheat the oven to 190°C/375°F/gas mark 5.

2 Trim the top leaves of the beetroot, leaving only about 5cm (2in) in place, then rinse and dry on kitchen paper. Transfer to a roasting tin (I find it easier to use a loaf tin to contain the beetroot securely). Drizzle over the oil, season and roll the beetroot around to coat.

3 Roast in the oven for 1 hour, or until a sharp knife easily pierces each root. Remove from the oven and set aside until cool enough to handle.

4 Wearing clean kitchen gloves to prevent staining your hands, slice off the top and the root of each beetroot, peel off the outer layer of skin, then slice each in half vertically – not quite to the bottom – then into quarters, then eighths. Each should open up like a segmented orange. Spoon crème fraîche on to each beetroot, sprinkle with chives and serve.

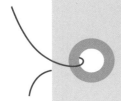

Perfect roast vegetables
Cut all your vegetables into similar-sized pieces for even cooking. The smaller the pieces, the quicker the roasting time. However, be prepared for hard root vegetables, such as potatoes and carrots, to take up to 1 hour, while soft vegetables, such as peppers or aubergines, should need just 20–30 minutes. Toss or drizzle the vegetables with plain olive oil (keep the expensive extra-virgin variety for dressings) and make sure they are evenly coated, then season. You can choose to add whole garlic cloves and robust herbs such as thyme or rosemary at this stage, if you like. Toss the vegetables once or twice during cooking so they roast evenly. They are done when tender (test with a small, sharp knife) and beginning to crisp at the edges.

Green beans with lemon & pancetta

It's not easy to get children to eat vegetables, but sweet green beans are a good place to start. The lemon here gives them a great zing, while the pancetta helps ensure they disappear in no time. As with all vegetables, never overcook green beans or they will be bitter and dull.

Serves 4 as a side dish
Preparation time 5 minutes
Cooking time 10 minutes

250g (9oz) green beans, trimmed and halved
75g (2¾oz) pancetta, cubed
2 tbsp pine nuts
finely grated zest of 1 unwaxed lemon
salt flakes and black pepper

1 Blanch the beans for a couple of minutes, then refresh (*see* secret, below), making sure they don't remain too firm or they will squeak when eaten.

2 Place a nonstick frying pan over a medium heat and fry the pancetta, stirring occasionally, until it has released its fat and is crispy and golden. Add the pine nuts and toss for 1–2 minutes more until they take on a toasted colour. Add the drained beans and heat through, mixing everything together. Finally, add the lemon zest, season to taste and serve.

Blanching vegetables

The term 'blanch' refers to quick cooking in boiling water. Bring a large pan of salted water to the boil over a high heat, then add the prepared vegetables. Boil for the time specified in the recipe, drain well and plunge into ice-cold water. This is called 'refreshing' the vegetables. Blanching helps to set the colour so, whether you choose to cook the vegetables further or not, they will always remain brightly coloured.

Cream cheese broad beans & garden peas

I use a light cream cheese for this recipe, but you should choose the type you like best. This is a great way of disguising healthy greens to make them more appealing to children, and is delicious with my Ricotta, Pepper & Artichoke Quiche (see page 130).

Serves 4 as a side dish
Preparation time 5 minutes,
    plus 30 minutes podding
Cooking time 5–10 minutes
Can be made in advance
Suitable for freezing

250g (9oz) broad beans (podded weight)
250g (9oz) garden peas (shelled weight)
1 tbsp olive oil
3–4 tbsp light cream cheese
25g (1oz) Parmesan cheese, finely grated
small handful of flatleaf parsley, chopped
salt flakes and black pepper

1 Blanch the broad beans for 2 minutes, refresh in ice-cold water (*see* secret, page 170), then remove the skin from each bean (*see* secret, below). Blanch the peas for 1 minute, then refresh them also.

2 Pour the olive oil into a pan over a medium-low heat, add the peas and broad beans and stir. Spoon in the cream cheese and sprinkle over the Parmesan, stirring to coat the beans and peas. Add the parsley and gently simmer for no more than a couple of minutes, adding a splash of water if needed to stop the mixture from drying out. Season to taste and serve immediately.

Double-podding broad beans
Towards the end of the season, when these beans are older and larger, they may need double-podding. This process gives an extra-tender broad bean. You need a little time and patience to do this, but it can be a relaxing process. Blanch the broad beans (*see* secret, page 170), then peel each one by squeezing it between your fingers. The outer skin will slip off to reveal the bright green bean beneath. Discard the outer skin.

Mangetout salad

Mangetout is an incredibly versatile vegetable. It is wonderful in salads and stir-fries, and can also serve as the 'greens' to go with any main meal. This dish tastes great with lots of different recipes, but it's especially good with Chinese-influenced flavours.

Serves 4 as a side dish
Preparation time 5 minutes
Cooking time 5 minutes

200g (7oz) mangetout, trimmed
1 tbsp olive oil
90g (3¼oz) fresh bean sprouts
salt flakes and black pepper
1 tbsp soy sauce

1 Blanch the mangetout for 2 minutes, then refresh in ice-cold water (*see* secret, page 170).

2 Pour the oil into a pan over a medium heat, toss in the mangetout and stir to heat through. Add the bean sprouts and heat through for a couple more minutes, stirring, then season, going easy on the salt as you will be adding soy sauce.

3 Drizzle with the soy sauce, then serve immediately.

Bean sprouts

In this recipe, the bean sprouts complement the mangetout perfectly, as both have a crisp bite that makes the salad very easy to eat. Available in bags in most supermarkets, bean sprouts can be used to add bulk and bite to stir-fries with noodles. They are highly nutritious, but if you eat them raw – as some seem to encourage – you miss out on their protein, which is released through cooking.

Curly kale with anchovies, onion & garlic

This dish would work equally well with savoy cabbage or spring greens, but, if you're using young, sweet spring greens, you won't need to cook them any further after you add them back to the pan. Instead, simply warm them through with the other ingredients.

Serves 4 as a side dish
Preparation time 5–10 minutes
Cooking time 15 minutes

200g (7oz) curly kale, trimmed
   (*see* secret, below)
2 tbsp olive oil
2 garlic cloves, finely sliced
1 large onion, finely sliced
3 tbsp red wine vinegar
3 canned anchovies, drained and
   finely chopped
salt flakes and black pepper

1 Blanch the kale for 1–2 minutes, then refresh in ice-cold water (*see* secret, page 170) and shake thoroughly to dry.

2 Pour the oil into a pan over a gentle heat and add the garlic and onion. Cook, stirring, for 2–3 minutes until softened. Add the vinegar and the anchovies and continue to fry for 2–3 minutes, then return the kale. Pour in 75–100ml (2½–3½fl oz) water to help steam the kale, and season well. Cook for 5–6 minutes, stirring, then serve immediately.

Tackling curly kale

Kale can be a baffling vegetable to prepare if you're unfamiliar with it, but it has a delicious strong taste and is very good for you. Choose a bright green bunch, wash it well and tear the frilly leaves from their tough central stalks. Larger leaves can be sliced or shredded if you want. This recipe is great, but try kale in a stir-fry or sauté as well. Bacon makes a wonderful addition.

Pan-fried corn on the cob

As a family we love corn on the cob. Megan, our eldest daughter, now has a dental brace and really misses it, so I invented these smaller versions that she can still manage. You can choose to barbecue this recipe if you prefer (see secret, below).

Serves 4 as a side dish
Preparation time 5 minutes
Cooking time 20 minutes

4 cobs of sweetcorn
salt flakes and black pepper
2 tbsp olive oil
50g (1¾oz) unsalted butter
10g (¼oz) fresh rosemary, finely chopped

1 Place the cobs into a pan of boiling salted water, bring back to the boil and simmer for 10 minutes; luckily, you can't really overcook them.

2 When the cobs are tender to the tip of a knife, drain them and set aside until cool enough to handle. Using a very sharp knife, slice each cob into rings of about 2.5cm (1in) thick and season.

3 Heat the oil in a frying pan and add the corn. You may have to do this in batches. Fry, turning, until the corn is golden on all sides, then add the butter and rosemary and spoon it over the rings (be careful of any spitting butter). Allow the corn to become a nice nutty golden colour.

4 Transfer the corn to a plate, pouring over the remaining butter and rosemary. Sprinkle over a little more salt and set aside until cool enough to pick up and eat. Serve warm.

Sweetcorn on the barbecue

If you'd like to try this recipe on the barbecue, simply follow the recipe to the end of step 2, then toss the rings in the oil. Wrap them in foil to prevent them from catching on the barbecue's flames and place the package on the barbecue for 5–10 minutes, turning once. The sweetcorn will pick up a lovely smoky flavour. Remove from the heat, then spoon the butter and rosemary into the package.

Stuffed mushrooms

This is great as a starter or side dish. The quantities are substantial, and it's excellent for vegetarians if you leave out the pancetta. Cooking the field mushrooms in the oven rather than in a frying pan means they retain all their juices.

Serves 4
Preparation time 15 minutes
Cooking time 35 minutes
Can be made in advance

8 field mushrooms, stalks removed and
   finely chopped
20g (¾oz) butter, cut into 8 cubes
1 garlic clove, finely chopped
1 tbsp finely chopped parsley
1 red onion, finely chopped
75g (2¾oz) pancetta, cubed
1 bay leaf
100ml (3½fl oz) white wine
2 tbsp crème fraîche
3 tbsp breadcrumbs (*see* secret, page 143)

1 Preheat the oven to 200°C/400°F/gas mark 6.

2 Clean the mushrooms (*see* secret, below). Place them, gills up, in an ovenproof dish and drop a knob of butter on to each. Bake for 20 minutes.

3 Meanwhile, in a small bowl, mix together the chopped mushroom stalks, garlic, parsley and onion. Fry the pancetta in a dry frying pan until it renders its fat, then add the mushroom stalk mix and allow it to soften for a minute. Throw in the bay leaf, then add the wine and leave to bubble and reduce for a couple of minutes. Turn the heat down, then stir through the crème fraîche. Take the pan off the heat and fish out the bay leaf.

4 Divide this stuffing between the mushrooms, then sprinkle over the breadcrumbs to add texture and colour. Return the mushrooms to the oven for a further 15 minutes, until golden brown.

How to clean mushrooms
Never rinse mushrooms with water or – worse still – plunge them into it, as they are like sponges and will soak the liquid up, rendering them tasteless and hard to cook successfully. Instead, wipe them either with damp kitchen paper or a soft brush reserved for the purpose, to remove any grit and soil. Many kitchen supply stores sell mushroom brushes expressly for this.

Asparagus soup

White or green asparagus can be used here, but green doesn't look as posh as white! To add texture to this dish, cut off the asparagus tips, make the soup as directed, then boil the tips in water for a minute, drain, chop into 5mm (¼in) lengths and place them in the bottom of the serving bowls, before pouring the soup on the top.

Serves 6 as a starter
Preparation time 10 minutes
Cooking time 10–15 minutes
Can be made in advance to end of step 2
Suitable for freezing at end of step 2

25g (1oz) unsalted butter, plus extra
   to butter the toast
2 shallots, finely sliced
750g (1lb 10oz) white (or green) asparagus,
   chopped into 2.5cm (1in) pieces
   (*see* secret, below)
1 litre (1¾ pints) good-quality, hot chicken
   stock (*see* secret, page 37)
2 tbsp crème fraîche
salt flakes and black pepper

To serve
toasted crusty white bread
few drops of truffle oil

1 Melt the butter in a large saucepan over a low heat and gently sauté the shallots for 2–3 minutes, or until softened but not coloured. Add the asparagus and cook, stirring, for 5–10 minutes, or until it begins to soften. Add the hot chicken stock and remove from the heat.

2 Pour the soup into a blender and process until smooth. You may have to do this in batches as the blender should be no more than half full each time to avoid an overspill; hold the lid on with a dish cloth to protect your hands from splashes.

3 Return the soup to the pan to warm through gently, stir in the crème fraîche and season to taste. Serve in warmed bowls, accompanied by buttered toast, topping with a drizzle of truffle oil and another pinch of black pepper.

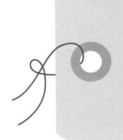

Choosing and preparing asparagus

You can find white asparagus in specialist greengrocers. It is white because it is grown under the soil and is slightly more tender and delicate in flavour than green asparagus. To trim asparagus spears, snap off and remove the woody stalk at the bottom; handily, it will break at the right place. You can discard these pieces or use as part of a vegetable stock. Thicker spears will need to be peeled of the tougher skin towards the base.

Celery soup

Soups are immensely comforting, but can also be impressive at a dinner party (with the added bonus that you can make them in advance). To ring the changes to this dish, try adding ½–1 teaspoon curry powder as you cook down the celery, or crumble a little Stilton over the top.

Serves 6
Preparation time 5–10 minutes
Cooking time 45–50 minutes
Can be made in advance to end of step 2
Suitable for freezing at end of step 2

100g (3½oz) butter
2 celery heads, trimmed, cut into
   2.5cm (1in) pieces
1.3 litres (2¼ pints) chicken stock
   (*see* secret, page 37)
75g (2¾oz) walnuts
125ml (4fl oz) double cream

1 Gently melt the butter in a large saucepan, then add the celery and its leaves. Allow to bubble, stirring occasionally, for 15–20 minutes, or until the celery is completely soft (*see* secret, below). Add the chicken stock and bring to the boil. Reduce the heat once more and simmer for another 15–20 minutes.

2 Add the walnuts and cook for 4–5 minutes, then transfer the soup to a blender and process until smooth. You may have to do this in batches as the blender should be no more than half full each time to avoid an overspill; hold the lid on with a dish cloth to protect your hands from splashes.

3 Stir in the double cream and return the soup to a clean pan over a medium heat until piping hot. Serve immediately.

The secret of perfect soup

With this or any other soup, there is an easy – though often overlooked – way to make the flavours sing. The key is patience. When starting a soup base, either with the celery in this recipe or more usually with onions, carrots and other aromatic roots, cook them gently in butter for a long time (at least 20 minutes) to intensify their tastes. Stir occasionally to prevent sticking.

Fresh green salad with bacon

This salad is simple, highly nutritious and very good to eat. Top with a poached egg to be extra fancy, or serve it with my Best-ever Homemade Chips (see page 164) on the side if it seems too healthy for you or you need a more substantial meal.

Serves 4 as a main course
Preparation time 15 minutes
Cooking time 10 minutes
Can be made in advance to end of step 3

150g (5½oz) peas (shelled weight)
150g (5½oz) broad beans (podded weight)
6 rashers of smoked bacon
4 handfuls of rocket
4 handfuls of baby spinach
2 endive heads, leaves separated
3 tbsp creamy mustard vinaigrette
  (see page 276)

How to make and dress a salad

Make sure all the leaves are very well washed and then meticulously dried. Damp leaves will never be crisp. Always apply the dressing at the last minute. This will ensure the leaves remain fresh and vibrant – adding the dressing too early will turn the salad limp and soggy. The dressing can be made in a clean jam jar. Place all the ingredients into the jar and, with the lid securely on, shake vigorously to combine. Any leftover dressing can be stored in the fridge.

1 Bring to the boil over a high heat a large pan of water that fits your steamer. Place the peas and broad beans in the steamer over the boiling water. Cover and cook for 3 minutes. Meanwhile, fill a large bowl with ice and water. Drain the cooked peas and beans, then plunge them immediately into the iced water to refresh (see secret, page 170). Drain again, and transfer them on to kitchen paper to dry.

2 Place a frying pan over a high heat. When it is hot, fry the bacon until crispy, then blot on kitchen paper to remove any excess fat. Allow to cool, then cut into strips.

3 Wash and dry the leaves, then place them in a large salad bowl with the peas, beans and bacon. If preparing in advance, cover with clingfilm and leave in the refrigerator for up to 2 hours. Remove from the refrigerator ahead of serving; nothing is more tasteless than 'fridge-cold' salad.

4 Just before serving, give the vinaigrette a good whisk and pour it over the salad, tossing well so all the ingredients are coated.

Chinese leaf & chilli salad

This fresh, clean-tasting, warm salad is great served alongside a rich and substantial meat dish; try it with my Marinated Duck Breasts (see page 63) for a delicious combination of flavours and textures. Be careful with the toasted sesame oil: it's strong and can be overpowering.

Serves 4 as a side dish
Preparation time 5–10 minutes
Cooking time 5 minutes

1 head of Chinese leaf, stem removed,
　thinly shredded
1 red chilli, seeds left in, finely sliced
　(*see* secret, below)
3 spring onions, sliced at an angle into
　5mm (¼in) pieces
1 tbsp toasted sesame oil
1 tbsp soy sauce
2 tbsp sesame seeds, toasted
salt flakes and black pepper

1 Place the Chinese leaf, chilli and spring onions in a large mixing bowl. Add the oil, soy sauce and sesame seeds and carefully mix everything together.

2 Place a deep frying pan over a medium heat. Add the salad along with 2 tbsp water to help steam the vegetables. Cook, stirring occasionally, for no more than 3 minutes, to retain a good crunch to the leaf. Season to taste and serve straight from the pan.

Chilli know-how

Generally speaking, the smaller the chilli, the hotter it is. As you prepare chillies, your skin will absorb their capsaicin, which gives a burning, throbbing sensation. Touching a chilli and then rubbing your eyes is not a pleasant experience, so be careful! To reduce the heat of any dish, remove chilli seeds and membrane with a teaspoon, as this is where the spicy chemical is found.

New potato salad
with crème fraîche & coriander

This is a classic and a dish you can keep in the refrigerator to use in everything from children's lunchboxes to a bits-and-pieces saturday family meal. It's a very adaptable recipe as well; try adding pieces of crispy bacon or your favourite soft herbs to jazz it up.

Serves 4 as a side dish
Preparation time 10 minutes
Cooking time 20–25 minutes
Can be made in advance

500g (1lb 2oz) Charlotte new potatoes,
   larger ones halved (*see* secret, below)
salt flakes and black pepper
1 tbsp olive oil
3 tbsp crème fraîche
4 spring onions, finely chopped
1 tbsp red wine vinegar
small handful of finely chopped coriander

1 Place the potatoes in a pan and cover with cold water, adding a pinch of salt. Bring to the boil and simmer for 20–25 minutes, until just tender to the tip of a knife.

2 Drain the potatoes and transfer into a mixing bowl. Drizzle over the oil and allow to cool for 10 minutes.

3 In a separate bowl, mix together the crème fraîche, spring onions and vinegar. Spoon this mixture into the bowl with the potatoes and gently toss, ensuring they are all covered. Season, then fold in the coriander. Serve at room temperature.

The best potatoes for salad

You will need waxy potatoes for salad, such as the Charlottes I use in this recipe, or you could try Anya or Ratte varieties, which are increasingly easy to find. These are firm enough not to break up in the dressing, especially if you take care to cook them only until just tender. Peel them after cooking if you wish, when their skins slip off easily, and dress while still warm so they absorb all the flavours.

A bit of dough

Easy handmade white bread · Pizza dough · Perfect pizza
Tomato & prosciutto bruschetta · Scones for the perfect afternoon tea

Secrets of preparing dough

Many people are scared of making bread. I started when I was training for a marathon with my good friend Jo. While running, we had long conversations about food. She swore by the bread machine that she uses religiously every day. I loved the thought of homemade bread, so I researched recipes I could make, simply, without a machine. Finally I came up with my Easy Handmade White Bread (*see* page 194) and I've used the recipe ever since. It's so much lighter than most loaves. And I was inspired by Jo's bread talk!

We have a rule in our house: if we buy sliced bread, we only ever get wholegrain. I never buy sliced white or long-life bread, but I always have an emergency loaf in the freezer.

When you make your own bread, you'll know exactly what's in it. Use a variety of seeds, such as pumpkin or sesame, or even add walnuts or raisins for a loaf that is wonderful with blue cheese.

You'll never regret learning to make pizza dough (*see* page 196). Children always love to eat whatever they have made themselves, and this is the perfect way to let them make their own dinner. Rustle up a batch of dough in the morning, wrap it in clingfilm and keep it in the refrigerator. It's so much easier than you might think.

Have a children's pizza party with my Perfect Pizza (*see* page 198). In our house, the rule is that the kids always have to have three 'nice' things (which means vegetables) before they indulge themselves with the less wholesome toppings! For adults, chuck on a handful of rocket when the pizza comes out of the oven.

Knowing how to make bruschetta (*see* page 200) will get you out of all sorts of fixes. Kids love it, and you can easily tweak the recipe to serve as a canapé at most adult gatherings. Try adding red wine to the tomatoes for a sophisticated twist, or add chopped chicken, fresh coriander, chilli and mango for an exotic bite.

Make my Scones for the Perfect Afternoon Tea (*see* page 202) for the children to eat when you have only half an hour between the end of school and the start of their swimming lessons. It's a nice way to tide them over until supper time.

Easy handmade white bread

I own a bread machine, but in all honesty it sits gathering dust and is pulled out only when I feel guilty for not using it! The only way I really enjoy making bread is by hand and in the simplest way possible. This recipe is so easy and quick, and the bread is really light.

Makes 2 × 450g (1lb) loaves
Preparation time 10–15 minutes,
   plus 1½–2 hours rising
Cooking time 40–45 minutes
Can be made in advance
Suitable for freezing

840g (1lb 13oz) strong white flour,
   plus extra to dust
2 × 7g sachets dried yeast
2 tbsp brown sugar
1 tbsp salt
sunflower oil, for the bowl

1 In a large bowl, mix together the flour, yeast, sugar and salt. Stir in 500ml (18fl oz) tepid water and mix into a soft dough. Using an electric mixer fitted with a dough hook, knead the dough for 5 minutes, or turn it on to a floured surface and knead well by hand for 10–15 minutes.

2 Place the dough in a large oiled bowl and cover with a damp, clean dish cloth or clingfilm. Leave in a warm place to rise for 1½–2 hours until doubled in size.

3 Knock back the dough, briefly knead again, then divide into 2 pieces. Shape each into a round loaf or other shape (*see* secret, below) and place on a floured baking sheet. Unless you are making a braid, score a cross in the top of each loaf with a sharp knife.

4 Place the bread in the middle of a cold oven and slide a pot of hot water into the bottom of the oven to create steam, which forms a crust. Turn the oven to 180°C/350°F/gas mark 4 and bake for 35 minutes, until golden. Once the loaves are cooked (*see* secret, below), transfer to a wire rack and allow to cool.

Shaping dough

Try making other shapes from dough. For a plait, split the dough into 3 equal-sized parts and roll each into a thin sausage. Pinch the ends together and braid the dough, tucking the other ends underneath. Alternatively, knot sausages of dough, or form them into breadsticks. Make smaller balls for baps, dusting with flour before baking. Smaller loaves need shorter baking times. To test if bread is cooked, tap on the bottom: a cooked loaf rings hollow.

Pizza dough

This is a simple recipe, so don't be afraid to tackle it. You can keep all the ingredients in your storecupboard and throw the dough together at very short notice for any occasion. Make it in the morning, then refrigerate for an afternoon children's pizza party.

Makes enough for 4 large pizzas
Preparation time 25 minutes,
   plus 1–2 hours rising
Can be made in advance

7g sachet dried yeast
2 tsp runny honey
2 tbsp extra virgin olive oil,
   plus extra for the bowl
550g (1lb 4oz) strong white flour,
   plus extra to dust
1 tsp salt
1 tsp ground black pepper

1 Pour 150ml (¼ pint) warm water into a bowl and stir in the yeast to dissolve. Leave in a warm place for 10 minutes. Add the honey and oil to the yeast and combine well.

2 Sift the flour, salt and pepper into a large mixing bowl. Make a well in the centre and add the yeast mixture, mixing until you have a soft, slightly sticky dough. Gradually add more warm water if needed, to achieve the right consistency.

3 Transfer the dough to a lightly floured surface and lightly flour your hands. Knead for 10 minutes, or until the dough is elastic and easy to handle.

4 Lightly oil a large mixing bowl that is big enough to allow the dough to rise. Put in the dough and cover with a damp, clean dish cloth or clingfilm. Leave in a warm place for 1–2 hours, until doubled in size.

5 Take out the dough and punch it down until smooth, kneading. Divide into 4 balls and leave, wrapped in clingfilm, in the refrigerator until ready to use.

Bread and warmth

Whether making pizza or bread dough, you must always use warm water. If it is too cold, the yeast will not activate; if too hot, you risk killing the yeast. Leave the dough to rise in a warm place to enable the yeast to continue making the bubbles in the dough that will give a light, airy result. An airing cupboard or warm kitchen counter is perfect.

Perfect pizza

I love pizza topped with the ingredients I describe here. But a pizza is a very personal thing, and is a great blank canvas. For an unusual topping that's a winner with everyone – especially children – try poaching chicken, cutting it into slices, then drizzling over some barbecue sauce.

Serves 1
Preparation time 10 minutes
Cooking time 10–15 minutes
Can be made in advance

1 ball of Pizza Dough (*see* page 196)
flour, to dust
6 tbsp Tomato Sauce (*see* page 278)
6 slices salami
12 canned anchovies in oil, drained
6 basil leaves, roughly chopped
2 tbsp finely grated Parmesan cheese

1 Preheat the oven to 230°C/450°F/gas mark 8, placing a heavy baking sheet inside.

2 Place the dough ball on a lightly floured work surface and form your pizza base (*see* secret, below). You want to end up with a base approximately ½cm (¼in) thick.

3 Lay the pizza base on a piece of greaseproof paper. Spoon on the tomato sauce, smoothing it right up to the edges. Arrange the salami over the pizza, followed by the anchovies and basil. Finish it off by sprinkling over the Parmesan.

4 Slide the pizza on to the hot baking sheet inside the oven and bake for 10–15 minutes, until crisp and golden.

Shaping pizza bases
Push your ball of dough flat, then pick it up and slap it on to a floured work surface a couple of times. Then either drape it over a clenched fist and stretch gently from the outside rim (you could even twirl it like the professionals do!) or just roll out with a rolling pin. If you prefer a slightly thicker base, reduce the oven temperature so the pizza cooks all the way through without burning on top.

Tomato & prosciutto bruschetta

These make a great starter, snack or light lunch, or even canapés for a drinks party (make them smaller and neater for that, though). Depending on the occasion and your palate, try topping with tomato, basil, mozzarella, anchovies or olives. The only limit is your imagination!

Serves 4 as a starter
Preparation time 5 minutes
Cooking time 15 minutes
Can be made in advance to end of step 2

1 tbsp olive oil, plus extra to drizzle
200g (7oz) baby plum tomatoes,
    sliced lengthways
½ tbsp oregano leaves
1 tbsp balsamic vinegar
salt flakes and black pepper
6 slices prosciutto
1 ciabatta loaf
1 garlic clove, halved
25g (1oz) Parmesan cheese, finely grated

1 Heat the oil in a frying pan and toss in the tomatoes to warm through and break down slightly. Add the oregano, balsamic vinegar and black pepper. Stir through, remove from the heat and allow to cool slightly.

2 Fry the prosciutto in a dry nonstick pan over a high heat until crispy and golden, then place on kitchen paper to blot off the excess oil.

3 Preheat the grill to its highest setting. Cut the ciabatta in half lengthways, then slice each half into 2 equal portions.

4 Drizzle olive oil over the cut side of each piece of ciabatta. Sprinkle over a little salt and place under the grill until golden brown. Rub with the garlic (*see* secret, below).

5 Crumble the prosciutto over the ciabatta slices, then spoon on the tomato mix and sprinkle with the Parmesan and some more black pepper. Serve hot.

Toast – nature's own grater!
It is astonishing how effectively a toasted slice of bread acts as a grater for garlic. Halve a garlic clove and rub the cut surface over the toast. The clove will begin to disappear as you do so, transferring all its aromatic pulp and juices to the bread. Try this before serving up mushrooms on toast and you'll never look back.

Scones for the perfect afternoon tea

These are perfect served slightly warm with clotted cream and jam. They do keep until the next day, but are best with the scent of the oven still dancing around them. Try to make them when you know the batch will be devoured in a single sitting – preferably not by you on your own!

Makes 9 scones
Preparation time 10–15 minutes
Cooking time 10–12 minutes
Can be made in advance
Suitable for freezing

280g (10oz) plain flour,
   plus extra to dust
good pinch of salt
2 tsp baking powder
120g (4oz) butter
50g (1¾oz) sultanas
1 free-range egg
100ml (3½fl oz) milk

To serve
strawberry jam
clotted cream

1 Preheat the oven to 200°C/400°F/gas mark 6.

2 Sift the flour with the other dry ingredients into a large bowl. Add the butter, cut into knobs, then rub it into the flour with your fingertips until the mixture resembles breadcrumbs. Stir in the sultanas.

3 Beat together the egg and milk, add to the flour mixture and stir through until it forms a dough. Knead lightly on a floured surface, then roll or pat the dough flat and, using a 5cm (2in) fluted round cutter, cut out your scones (*see* secret, below).

4 Place the scones on an oven tray lined with greaseproof paper and bake for 10–12 minutes or until lightly golden. Leave to cool slightly, then serve as soon as possible.

5 Serve each scone cut in half and topped with spoonfuls of strawberry jam and clotted cream.

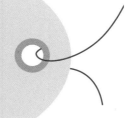

Perfect scones

Handle the dough gently, work quickly and do not over-knead or the scones will be chewy and stodgy. Don't roll (or pat out) the dough any thinner than 2cm (¾in) or you will end up with biscuits. Flour the cutter before you cut out the scones: this will prevent the dough from sticking to it and help the scones rise more evenly.

Something sweet

Meringues · Eton mess · Blackberry ice cream · Coconut sorbet
Orange sorbet · Raspberry sorbet · Melon cooler · Frozen fruit
Pineapple with a lime twist · Mango & passion fruit dessert
Caramelised peaches with hazelnut crème fraîche
Apricot, raspberry & ginger crumble · Plum & almond pudding
Pear & ginger steamed sponge pudding · Homemade ginger lemonade
Cherry & chocolate mousse · Chocolate cheesecake
simple Champagne cocktail

Secrets of making desserts

As a family we eat a lot of fruit, especially during summer when I don't want fatty food. On a sunny day, when the children are playing in the paddling pool and Gordon and I are drinking a glass of wine in the garden, we all want something light to snack on. So I prepare a platter of fruit and a bowl of strawberries with chopped mint and a sprinkling of balsamic vinegar, which makes a fantastic combination. Try it!

Though I love desserts, we don't have them from Monday to Friday. They are a weekend treat. Since I've taken up running, I don't have to worry about eating them. These days I run further and eat more!

When I go shopping with the children they are always drawn to the beautiful, intriguing pineapples and they want me to buy them. So I developed my Pineapple with a Lime Twist (*see* page 222). It's something nice to do with a pineapple that isn't doesn't involve skewering chunks on cocktail sticks! It feels exotic and is very welcome on a summer day.

The only fruit I have all year round – because I've heard they are great brain food – is blueberries. They are a pick-me-up, giving a little sunshine on those dull days.

Frozen Fruit (*see* page 221) is my new craze. I started making it after a friend instructed me to try freezing red grapes. They were a revelation – when you bite into them it's like a lovely sorbet in the centre. They are so nice to serve after a meal, while you are finishing your wine. Remove from the fridge 10 minutes before serving to take the frozen edge off them, and present in little bowls. The kids adore them, too.

Sorbets and ice creams are not an everyday treat, but if we have people coming to dinner, I make double so we have some left in the freezer for the family. I haven't got an ice cream machine; you don't need one either.

Crumbles (*see* page 226) are my favourite pudding. When making them, concentrate on really good-quality fruit and simply prepare it in the old-fashioned way. Never over-complicate it. A spoonful of crumble in a bowl rather than something restauranty that's been meticulously tweaked is my idea of dessert heaven.

Meringues

The secret to perfect meringue is to cook it as slowly as possible on a low heat. My mum used to leave them in the coolest oven of her Aga to cook overnight. Remember that you are not baking them so much as drying them out.

Makes 20 meringues of 5cm (2in) diameter
Preparation time 25 minutes
Cooking time 5 hours
Can be made in advance
Suitable for freezing for up to 1 month

4 large free-range egg whites
1 tbsp lemon juice
175g (6oz) caster sugar

Perfect meringues

Use an immaculately clean glass, china or stainless-steel bowl when making meringues; avoid plastic, as it may retain grease, which makes it hard to whip the egg whites. Make sure you do not have any yolk in the egg white as, again, the fat will prevent it from whisking properly. Use eggs at room temperature (older eggs are best, rather than fresh) as they whisk better than cold eggs. The meringue has been whipped enough when you can hold the bowl upside down without it falling out! Bake meringues at a low temperature to stop them from browning and cool them slowly in the oven to minimise cracking. Keep in an airtight container for up to a week.

1 Preheat the oven to 100°C/200°F/gas mark ¼.

2 Place the egg whites in a clean mixing bowl, ensuring all your utensils are spotless and dry. If you have an electric whisk, use it, otherwise you are going to need very strong arms! Whisk the egg whites until they are foamy, then increase the speed, add the lemon juice and whisk until the mixture is stiff enough to form peaks when the whisk is removed. Add the sugar and give a final whisk to combine. The mixture should be glossy.

3 Line a baking sheet with greaseproof paper. Spoon small 1 tbsp portions of the meringue on to the baking sheet, using a whipping action with the spoon each time to form a peak on top of each. The meringues should be about 5cm (2in) in diameter.

4 Transfer the meringues to the oven and bake slowly for 5 hours. They are ready when they can be lifted easily off the greaseproof paper and sound hollow when tapped gently underneath. Turn off the oven and leave the meringues inside until they have cooled completely.

Eton mess

This is one of my favourite desserts. I adore the different textures: the brittle, dry meringue surrounded by creaminess and fruit. I'd even go as far as to say it's better than chocolate! For extra crunch, sprinkle the top with chopped pistachios or hazelnuts.

Serves 6
Preparation time 15 minutes
Can be made in advance

450g (1lb) strawberries, hulled
1 tbsp icing sugar
570ml (1 pint) double cream
½ recipe meringues (*see* page 208)

1 Cut all the strawberries in half, then put half of them into a blender with the icing sugar. Process until smooth (*see* secret, below) and set aside.

2 In a large mixing bowl, whip the double cream until thickened, but not stiff. Fold in the remaining strawberries. Carefully break the meringues into pieces and fold them in until all is evenly mixed.

3 Drizzle most of the strawberry purée into the mix, folding through casually until the mixture is streaked throughout, then serve in dessert glasses drizzled with the reserved purée.

Beautifying Eton mess
Be careful to fold in the strawberry purée slowly and don't over-work the mixture as you want to create a striking 'ripple' effect. For a smoother finish, the strawberry purée can be strained through a sieve to remove any seeds.

Blackberry ice cream

This is heaven. You can't easily find this flavour in the shops, and it's one that takes me back to my childhood. I would often go blackberrying and, in the autumn, would collect an abundance of the fruits. The kids love this ice cream, too, especially as it stains their tongues purple!

Makes about 1 litre (1¾ pints)
Preparation time 30 minutes,
    plus overnight freezing
Cooking time 10–12 minutes
Can be made in advance

450g (1lb) blackberries
2 tbsp runny honey
50g (2oz) caster sugar
400ml can evaporated milk
150ml (5fl oz) double cream, whipped
3 tbsp lemon juice

1 Place the blackberries, honey and sugar into a medium saucepan. Cook gently over a low heat for 10–12 minutes, or until the blackberries are soft and slightly mushy. Transfer the mixture to a blender and process until smooth. Pass through a sieve into a clean bowl and allow to cool.

2 Meanwhile, in another large bowl, whip the evaporated milk until slightly thickened. Fold in the cream, blackberry purée and lemon juice.

3 Pour the mixture into a plastic container and place in the freezer for 45 minutes, or until it is beginning to freeze around the edges. Remove, transfer to a chilled bowl (or the bowl of a food processor) and beat until smooth and creamy. Repeat this freezing and beating process twice more (*see* secret, below), then return to the freezer until ready to serve. If using an ice-cream machine, churn for 1 hour instead, then turn into a lidded plastic container and store in the freezer.

Making ice creams and sorbets without an ice-cream machine

If you don't have an ice-cream machine you can still make wonderful sorbets and ice creams, but you must beat the mixture – by hand or in a food processor – 3 times during the freezing process. This avoids the formation of ice crystals and creates a smoother result. Place the sorbet or ice-cream container (such as a plastic tub) in the freezer before you add the mixture, as it will help speed up the process, and do the same with the bowl in which you intend to beat the mixture.

Coconut sorbet

This is wonderful served alongside my Pineapple Tart Tatin (see page 145). It is something a bit different and reminds me of summer, especially with a bit of coconut liqueur poured over the top. I'm a huge sorbet fan; they are light and delicious and an excellent way to satisfy sweet cravings.

Makes about 1 litre (1¾ pints)
Preparation time 30 minutes,
    plus overnight freezing
Cooking time 5 minutes
Can be made in advance

250g (9oz) caster sugar
400ml can coconut milk
1 tsp glycerine

1 Put the sugar into a pan with 400ml (14fl oz) cold water. Place over a medium heat until all the sugar has dissolved, then set aside for 30 minutes to cool.

2 Whisk the coconut milk to remove any lumps, then pour it into the cooled sugar syrup along with the glycerine.

3 Pour the mixture into a plastic container and place in the freezer for 45 minutes, or until it is beginning to freeze around the edges. Remove, transfer to a chilled bowl (or the bowl of a food processor) and beat until smooth and creamy. Repeat this freezing and beating process twice more (*see* secret, page 212), then return to the freezer until ready to serve. If using an ice-cream machine, churn for 1 hour instead, then turn into a lidded plastic container and store in the freezer.

4 Remove from the freezer at least 10 minutes before serving to soften slightly, for maximum flavour.

Incredible coconut milk
What did we do before we could buy canned coconut milk? It is a truly essential item in my storecupboard. It is wonderfully versatile, adding succulence to curries, a beautiful nutty taste to basmati rice and, of course, its delicious flavour to this sorbet recipe. It always needs to be whisked before use, as it often separates in the can into a thick paste and a watery liquid.

Orange sorbet

Sorbets are fantastically refreshing puddings that satisfy a sweet craving without making you feel overloaded – and they are much easier to make than you might think, even without an ice-cream machine. Give it a try and it will soon become part of your regular repertoire.

Makes about 1.2 litres (2 pints)
Preparation time 30 minutes,
    plus overnight freezing
Cooking time 5 minutes
Can be made in advance

250g (9oz) caster sugar
finely grated zest of 2 unwaxed oranges
750ml (1 pint 9fl oz) fresh orange juice
juice of 1 lemon

1 Put the sugar into a pan with 250ml (9fl oz) cold water. Place over a medium heat until all the sugar has dissolved. Add the orange zest, remove from the heat and set aside to cool for 30 minutes.

2 Strain the mixture through a sieve to remove the orange zest, then add the orange and lemon juice. Stir together, pour the mixture into a plastic container and place in the freezer for 45 minutes, or until it is beginning to freeze around the edges. Remove, transfer to a chilled bowl (or the bowl of a food processor) and beat until smooth and creamy. Repeat this freezing and beating process twice more (*see* secret, page 212), then return to the freezer until ready to serve. If using an ice-cream machine, churn for 1 hour instead, then turn into a lidded plastic container and store in the freezer.

3 Remove from the freezer at least 10 minutes before serving to soften slightly, for maximum flavour.

Organising the freezer
Label all the items in your freezer with a marker pen or sticky labels; there's nothing worse than removing what you think is a delicious sorbet from the freezer 5 minutes before eating, then realising – too late – that it is a batch of chicken stock! Try to make sure that plastic freezer containers are kept for either sweet or savoury items to minimise the risk of aromas and tastes migrating. Onion-flavoured sorbet, anybody…?

Raspberry sorbet

I have suggested using raspberries in this recipe, but you can use strawberries or blackberries instead, depending on the season. It is not necessary to strain the raspberry purée, as I do in step 2 — it just depends on how you feel about pips...

Makes about 1.2 litres (2 pints)
Preparation time 30 minutes,
   plus overnight freezing
Cooking time 5 minutes
Can be made in advance

300g (10½oz) caster sugar
finely grated zest and juice of
   1 unwaxed lemon
900g (2lb) raspberries

1 Put the sugar into a pan with 250ml (9fl oz) cold water and the lemon zest. Place over a medium heat until all the sugar has dissolved, then remove from the heat. Strain to remove the lemon zest.

2 Place 850g (1lb 14oz) of the raspberries in a blender and process to a purée, then strain to remove the pips. Add the purée to the syrup. Crush the remaining raspberries and add them too; I don't strain these as I like a few pips in my sorbet. Add the lemon juice, stir, then set aside for 30 minutes to cool.

3 Pour the mixture into a plastic container and place in the freezer for 45 minutes, or until it is beginning to freeze around the edges. Remove, transfer to a chilled bowl (or the bowl of a food processor) and beat until smooth and creamy. Repeat this freezing and beating process twice more (*see* secret, page 212), then return to the freezer until ready to serve. If using an ice-cream machine, churn for 1 hour instead, then turn into a lidded plastic container and store in the freezer.

4 Remove from the freezer at least 10 minutes before serving to soften slightly, for maximum flavour.

Scooping sorbet and ice cream
Move sorbet to the refrigerator to soften for 10 minutes before serving; move ice cream 20 minutes beforehand. When you're ready to eat, place 2 ice-cream scoops in a bowl of just-boiled water, as a warm scoop will both glide through sorbet or ice cream and release its load more readily. Using one, form an even ball. Place the ball in a dish or cone, then drop the used scoop back into the bowl of water and pick up the other scoop to continue.

Melon cooler

This is a very unusual dessert – a bit like a posh smoothie. If you are serving it to children, pour the melon 'soup' into a mug, with the lovely strawberry salad at the bottom, and give them a teaspoon. This recipe makes a really fabulous end to a meal on a warm day.

Serves 2–4
Preparation time 15 minutes

1 ripe melon, Charentais or similar,
   with orange flesh
6 basil leaves
100g (3½oz) crème fraîche
200g (7oz) natural low-fat yogurt
2 ice cubes
4 large strawberries, cut into wedges
10g (¼oz) mint, finely chopped
finely grated zest and juice of
   1 unwaxed lime

1 Slice the melon in half and scoop out and discard the seeds. Remove the skin from one half, cut the flesh into chunks and place in a food processor with the basil, crème fraîche, yogurt and ice cubes. Whizz until smooth. Transfer to a jug and chill in the refrigerator until ready to serve.

2 Meanwhile, using a melon baller, make about 10 balls from the remaining melon. In a bowl mix together the strawberries and melon balls, most of the mint, the lime juice and most of the zest. Gently stir, taking care not to crush the strawberries.

3 Place a mound of fruit salad in a shallow bowl and gently pour the chilled melon 'soup' around the outside. Finish by sprinkling with the remaining mint and zest.

Choosing melons

This recipe is worth making when you have a really tasty, wonderfully aromatic, ripe melon. Always smell a melon before you buy it to get a whiff of that wonderful scented muskiness. If there's no perfume, there will be no flavour. The best time of year to find perfectly ripe, sweet fruits is the summer, so eat this when the weather is hot and you're feeling frazzled.

Frozen fruit

This is my new favourite snack; it saves you from diving into packets of crisps and is totally healthy! Frozen fruits are also an amazing after-dinner treat that will prevent you from reaching for yet more chocolates. Try this refreshing and zingy recipe once and you may find that you're totally hooked, too.

Serves 4 as a snack
Preparation time 10 minutes
Can be made in advance

150g (5½oz) red grapes
100g (3½oz) blueberries
2 satsumas, segmented
150g (5½oz) pineapple, cubed

1 Freeze the fruit (*see* secret, below), then mix it up and put it into freezer bags in snack-sized portions. Return to the freezer.

2 Remove the fruit from the freezer 10 minutes before eating, so it is not rock-hard. Simple as that!

How to freeze fruit
Freezing fruit maintains most of its nutritional value (and means you can enjoy seasonal treasures such as gooseberries all year round). For the best results, place your prepared fruit in a single layer on a tray, cover with clingfilm and place, flat, into the freezer. This way, the fruit will freeze individually and not stick together. When it is frozen solid, transfer the fruit into freezer bags for storage.

Pineapple with a lime twist

This guilt-free, easier-than-simple dessert takes minimum time and effort yet is cool, refreshing and delicious! It's a great dish to serve with afternoon cocktails, or as a palate cleanser after a heavy, rich meal. Leave out the chilli if you are serving this to children.

Serves 6
Preparation time 5–10 minutes
Can be made in advance

1 pineapple
finely grated zest and juice of
    1 unwaxed lime
½ red chilli, deseeded and very
    finely chopped

1 Prepare the pineapple and cut into ½–1cm (¼–½in) slices (*see* secret, below).

2 Arrange the pineapple slices on a plate. Sprinkle over the lime zest and chilli, then squeeze over the lime juice. Cover and keep in the refrigerator for up to 24 hours before use. Remember to bring the pineapple to room temperature before serving.

Choosing and preparing pineapples

Buy your fruit perfectly ripe. Colour is not always a sign of ripeness, so instead check the base: when pressed with a thumb it should 'give' a little. Also, look at the leaves: if you can easily pull a leaf away from the fruit, it is ripe. To prepare the pineapple, cut off the stalk and base. Stand the pineapple upright on its newly flat base and remove the tough, leathery skin using a sharp knife – I find a serrated breadknife useful. Then cut out all the 'eyes' – the regular indentations of hard skin – and cut the flesh into slices or chunks, as preferred. If the central core is hard, cut it out from each slice and discard.

Mango & passion fruit dessert

It doesn't get any simpler or tastier than this. You could try this dessert with a light sorbet on the side if you wanted to jazz it up a bit, but I think it is truly refreshing left as it is.

Serves 4
Preparation time 10 minutes
Can be made in advance

1 large ripe mango, peeled and thinly sliced
  (*see* secret, below)
4 passion fruit
finely grated zest of 2 unwaxed limes
10 mint leaves, finely chopped

1 Divide the mango slices between 4 serving plates. Halve the passion fruit, scoop out the pulp and seeds and drizzle them over the mango.

2 Sprinkle over the lime zest and mint, then serve.

Preparing mangoes

This is easy once you get the hang of it. Each mango has an oval, flat stone. Pick up the fruit and look at the stem end: the stone runs along the longest axis. Cut either side of the stone to remove the 2 'cheeks' of the mango, then peel it. The remaining flesh clinging to the stone is a harder prospect: just hack away as much of it as you can! Work over a bowl, to catch the lovely juices.

Caramelised peaches with hazelnut crème fraîche

This is a simple but impressive dessert that you can pretty much produce from storecupboard ingredients – you can even use canned peaches! For a nice change, roll the peach segments in flaked, toasted almonds at the end of step 2 and serve with plain crème fraîche.

Serves 4
Preparation time 10 minutes
Cooking time 10–15 minutes

50g (1¾oz) caster sugar
15g (½oz) unsalted butter
3 peaches, stoned, each cut into 6 wedges
100ml (3½fl oz) white wine

To serve
3 tbsp crème fraîche
50g (1¾oz) lightly toasted hazelnuts, chopped

1 Pour the sugar into a pan set over a medium heat and allow it to caramelise, watching constantly so it doesn't burn (*see* secret, page 145). Add the butter, keeping the pan moving until it is melted and you have a lovely rich brown glossy liquid.

2 Add the peach segments and toss so they are all coated with the caramel, then pour in the wine, allowing the liquid to bubble and reduce by half.

3 Meanwhile mix the crème fraîche with the chopped hazelnuts.

4 Divide the peach segments between 4 small serving bowls, drizzling a spoonful of their liquid over the top. Serve accompanied by the hazelnut crème fraîche.

How to toast nuts

Pour your nuts into a dry frying pan over a medium heat. Stir and toss them, so all sides are evenly roasted, watching constantly as they can scorch in an instant and become acrid. When they are ready they will smell delicious and appear golden brown. Transfer them to a plate to cool before serving; if you leave them in their pan they may well burn in the residual heat.

Apricot, raspberry & ginger crumble

When I was at school crumbles were my favourite desserts, and they have been ever since. This is a great way to use up over-ripe fruit. When you are feeling naughty, pour custard over the top, or serve with a spoon of ice cream, or even crème fraîche.

Serves 4–6
Preparation time 15 minutes
Cooking time 40–45 minutes
Can be made in advance
Suitable for freezing

50g (1¾oz) unsalted butter
700g (1lb 9oz) apricots, halved and stoned
leaves from 2 thyme sprigs
50g (1¾oz) caster sugar
175g (6oz) raspberries

For the crumble
175g (6oz) plain flour
80g (3oz) light brown sugar
½ tsp ground ginger
½ tsp ground cloves
½ tsp ground cinnamon
40g (1½oz) hazelnuts, chopped
75g (2¼oz) unsalted butter

1 Preheat the oven to 180°C/350°F/gas mark 4.

2 Melt the butter in a large frying pan over a low heat and add the apricots and thyme. Toss to coat in the butter and leave to heat through for a couple of minutes. Stir in the caster sugar and leave to bubble gently for 10–15 minutes, or until the apricots are softened but not breaking down.

3 Transfer the apricots to an ovenproof dish and sprinkle the raspberries evenly over the top.

4 Mix together all the dry ingredients for the crumble in a large bowl, add the butter, cut into knobs, and rub with your fingertips until the mixture resembles breadcrumbs. Sprinkle the crumble over the top of the fruit.

5 Place the crumble dish on a baking sheet and cook in the oven for 30 minutes, until golden and bubbling.

Saving apricots

Very sadly, unless you live close to where apricots are grown, you are likely to come across only disappointing fruits with a dry, woolly texture. Some, by contrast, will be mouth-puckeringly acidic. But you can save them by baking them, as in this recipe, or poaching them in a rosewater-flavoured syrup and serving with raspberry sauce. They can even be made into chutney.

Plum & almond pudding

This recipe works well with cherries, rhubarb or apple instead of plums, or you could even use canned or frozen fruit. Change the fruit to suit the season, your budget and your tastes, ringing the changes often for a bit of variety. Serve with vanilla ice cream, or just dig in as it is.

Serves 6
Preparation time 10 minutes
Cooking time 40–50 minutes

25g (1oz) butter
8 plums, stoned and cut into quarters
75g (2¾oz) light brown muscovado sugar
3 free-range eggs
100g (3½oz) caster sugar
75g (2¾oz) self-raising flour
75g (2¾oz) ground almonds
250ml (9fl oz) semi-skimmed milk
few drops of almond extract
2 tbsp flaked almonds

1 Preheat the oven to 180°C/350°F/gas mark 4.

2 Melt the butter in a large frying pan over a medium heat, add the plums and muscovado sugar and cook for 6–8 minutes until the plums have softened. Transfer the plums and their juices to a 2-litre (3½-pint) ovenproof dish, making sure there's enough room for the fruit to lie in a single layer.

3 Meanwhile, whisk the eggs and caster sugar together until pale in colour and thick enough for the whisk to leave a trail on the surface. Carefully beat in the flour, ground almonds, milk and almond extract. Spoon the mixture over the plums and sprinkle with the flaked almonds.

4 Bake in the oven for 35–40 minutes, or until the pudding is golden brown and set. After 20 minutes, check the top has not coloured too much; if it has, cover it with foil and return to the oven for the remaining cooking time.

Respect the seasons
When making this or any other fruit pudding, select your fruit to suit the season. Seasonal fruit will be the ripest and at the peak of its flavour. It will also be sold at its most economical price.

Pear & ginger steamed sponge pudding

This takes a while to cook, so prepare it in advance and leave it to putter away on the stove. Despite what you may imagine, this is a light dessert (though it is also wonderfully syrupy around the rim – that's the bit to fight over!). Perfect served with custard, or just on its own.

Serves 6
Preparation time 20 minutes
Cooking time 2 hours 10 minutes

knob of butter
2 tbsp caster sugar
2 ripe pears, peeled, cored and diced
100ml (3½fl oz) Calvados
30g (1oz) crystallised ginger, finely chopped
175g (6oz) unsalted butter, softened,
   plus extra for the basin
175g (6oz) granulated sugar
3 large free-range eggs, beaten
175g (6oz) self-raising flour

1 Place a sauté pan over a medium heat, add the butter and caster sugar and toss in the diced pears to coat. Standing well back, pour in the Calvados. Then add the ginger, stir and allow to bubble for 5 minutes. Transfer the pears to a plate and set aside to cool.

2 Cream together the butter and granulated sugar, using the paddle attachment of an electric mixer or by hand (follow the instructions in the secret, page 246). Add the eggs a little at a time, beating after each addition, then fold in the flour with the cooled pears.

3 Butter a 1.7-litre (3-pint) pudding basin well. Spoon in the batter and smooth off the top. Steam for up to 2 hours (*see* secret, below), making sure to top up the water so the pan does not run dry. To serve, turn out the sponge on to a plate.

How to steam a pudding

Cut both a piece of foil and a piece of greaseproof paper bigger than the top of the pudding basin (or just use a double thickness of greaseproof paper). Put them together and pleat the centre so the pudding has room to expand. Butter the paper and place it and the foil over the basin, buttered paper side down, tie string around to secure and make 2 string handles so the pudding is easier to remove from the steamer. Place a steamer over a pan of boiling water and lower in the pudding. Cover with a tight-fitting lid.

Homemade ginger lemonade

A good way to come across as the perfect mother is to turn up for the school sports day with homemade lemonade...it's very Famous Five! For an extra kick, serve with a shot of vodka (maybe not on sports day, though!).

Serves 6
Preparation time 10 minutes,
  plus 4 hours infusing
Can be made in advance

8cm (3¼in) fresh root ginger,
  peeled and very finely sliced
juice of 6 lemons, plus 1 unwaxed lemon,
  thinly sliced
90g (3¼oz) granulated sugar
handful of fresh mint leaves

1 Place the ginger, lemon juice, sliced lemon and sugar in a tall heatproof jug and add 1.5 litres (2¾ pints) boiling water. Stir and leave to cool, then cover and transfer to the refrigerator to infuse for at least 4 hours, or for as long as possible.

2 When the lemonade is ready to serve, pass the mixture through a sieve into a clean jug. Dilute with an equal part of water and serve with plenty of ice and the mint leaves.

How to choose and juice a lemon

Look for unwaxed lemons – this is very important if you are going to use the zest – with smooth, oily skins. They should be heavy for their size as the weightiest fruits will contain the most juice. Whole lemons will keep for 1–2 weeks at room temperature, but longer in the refrigerator. To extract the most juice from a fruit, use your palm to roll it firmly on a hard surface to loosen the fibres within. If you need only a little juice, pierce the end of the fruit with a fork, squeeze out the amount needed, wrap the remaining lemon in clingfilm and pop it back in the refrigerator for later.

Cherry & chocolate mousse

This is an easily impressive, light and airy dessert that you can whip up in advance. I use fresh cherries in this recipe, but I've also had a great deal of success with canned fruits when they're out of season, so don't just keep this dish for the summer months.

Makes 6 cocktail glasses
Preparation time 15 minutes,
   plus 30 minutes chilling
Cooking time 10 minutes
Can be made in advance

150g (5½oz) granulated sugar
400g (14oz) cherries, halved and stoned

For the mousse
140g (5oz) dark chocolate, plus extra
   to grate on top
500ml (18fl oz) half-fat crème fraîche
250ml (9fl oz) double cream,
   whipped to soft peaks

1 Put the sugar into a pan with 125ml (4fl oz) cold water. Place over a gentle heat until all the sugar has dissolved. Toss in the cherries, increase the heat and boil for about 5 minutes, or until the juices are syrupy and they coat the cherries. Transfer the cherries and juices into a bowl and set aside to cool.

2 Meanwhile, melt the chocolate (follow the instructions in the secret, below), then allow it to cool slightly. Gently stir in the crème fraîche and double cream.

3 Divide the cherry mixture between 6 cocktail glasses. Spoon the chocolate mousse on top of each and refrigerate for at least 30 minutes to chill and slightly set. Grate over a little more chocolate just before serving.

How to melt chocolate

Break the chocolate into chunks and place it in a heatproof bowl fitted over a pan of simmering water over a gentle heat, making sure the base of the bowl doesn't touch the water. Stir the chocolate only now and again and allow it to melt gently. If it becomes grainy or separates (known as 'seizing'), it has been over-heated. To rescue it, stir in 1 tsp vegetable oil.

Chocolate cheesecake

This is simple, delicious and very quick. Don't be worried that it might take you all day and involve using all the mixing bowls you own. Give it a go and it will soon become part of your regular repertoire.

Serves 8–10
Preparation time 15 minutes
Cooking time 1 hour
Can be made in advance

300g packet sweetened oat biscuits
75g (2¾oz) butter, melted
150g (5½oz) good-quality dark chocolate,
    broken into squares
750g (1lb 10oz) mascarpone or cream cheese
125g (4½oz) light brown muscovado sugar
3 free-range eggs, beaten

1 Preheat the oven to 180°C/350°F/gas mark 4. Line a 23cm (9in) non-stick springform tin with greaseproof paper.

2 Put the biscuits in a food processor and whizz until they are in fine crumbs (or put them in a polythene bag, seal and bash with a rolling pin). Place them in a large bowl, add the butter and stir until they are evenly coated. Transfer to the lined tin and press firmly with the back of a spoon to compress in an even layer over the base. Cover with clingfilm and put in the refrigerator for 10–15 minutes, until hardened.

3 Meanwhile, melt the chocolate (*see* secret, page 233). Remove from the heat and set aside to cool.

4 Put the mascarpone or cream cheese in another mixing bowl and, with a whisk, beat until loose and smooth. Add the sugar and beat again. Gently stir in the cooled chocolate and the eggs, then add this chocolate filling on to the chilled biscuit base.

5 Gently slide the cheesecake into the oven and bake for 50–60 minutes. When it's ready, it should still have a wobble to the centre if you shake the tin (it will continue to cook as it cools). Allow to cool completely, then refrigerate until ready to serve.

Why use brown sugar?
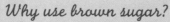
In this recipe I use light brown muscovado, which is a truly delicious sugar. It has a treacly flavour, which comes from the molasses syrup clinging to the grains. Refined white sugar has a less interesting taste, as all this molasses has been removed, so it is simply sweet without much depth. Use muscovado sugar when you can, to give your puddings real depth of flavour.

Simple Champagne cocktail

Champagne comes from the eponymous French region and is the classic choice for this drink, but use more economical sparkling wine here if you want to. Just be careful that it's a well-selected bottle, taking advice from a trusted wine merchant, to avoid cheap plonk.

Serves 4–6
Preparation time 5 minutes

2 passion fruits
1 bottle of your favourite Champagne
   or sparkling wine, chilled

1 Cut the passion fruits in half and scrape out all the seeds and pulp into a bowl.

2 Spoon 1 tsp passion fruit seeds into the bottom of each Champagne glass and divide the juices between them as well.

3 Pour Champagne over the passion fruit and serve immediately.

The right shape for Champagne glasses

Although the shallow, wide bowl of a Champagne coupe is attractive and remains popular in television costume dramas, it is really not the best vessel for your Champagne cocktail. A tall, slim flute will keep the drink fizzier, as the smaller surface area means there is less room for the bubbles to rise and escape. A flute will also save you the embarrassment of spluttering after bubbles have gone up your nose!

Cakes & biscuits

Raspberry & lemon torta · Victoria sponge · Cherry & almond loaf
Cupcake party time · Chocolate heaven cupcakes
Garibaldi biscuits · Apple & raspberry crumble muffins
Carrot & raisin cupcakes · Chocolate, fruit & nut cookies
Lemon & thyme shortbread · Gingerbread men & hearts

Secrets of baking cakes & biscuits

A lot of people are coming back to baking. As long as you follow the rules and measure things out accurately, it's easy. And you'll know exactly what your family is eating when you've made the cakes yourself. It's a really homely, satisfying feeling to bake your own.

I love making biscuits and that's the sort of home baking I do the most. I tend to make three times the recipe and store the dough in sausage-shapes wrapped in clingfilm in the refrigerator or freezer. This way, it takes an instant to impress people with freshly baked biscuits when they come to visit, or welcome the kids home to the smell of baking on a Friday evening.

Be brave and use unusual combinations of flavours in your baking. My Lemon & Thyme Shortbread (*see* page 264), for instance, may sound eccentric, but it tastes divine. Try the recipe with cinnamon instead, or even very finely chopped rosemary. You should always experiment in the kitchen, but don't be afraid to raise your hands and admit that something was a terrible combination and never try it again!

Having experienced the pressures of the mothers' competition at school cake sales, I have decided that the only way to go is to find a recipe that no-one else will know or, at least, to claim that what you have brought along is a unique cake. That way no one can say theirs is better than yours, or that you have messed up the baking!

Cupcakes (*see* pages 250, 254 and 260) will get you out of all sorts of holes. You can make them as glamorous as you like for a tea party, create individual cakes for each child, or even get the children to make their own designs. Just remember they are best eaten on the day they are made.

Muffins (*see* pages 257) are amazingly handy, and are a good breakfast on the run for you or your children.

Raspberry & lemon torta

This torta is at its delicious best when served slightly warm. It does sink a little in the middle but this recipe is all about taste, not looks. It will last a couple of days, which is always handy. And I do love raspberries!

Serves 8
Preparation time 10 minutes
Cooking time 1 hour
Can be made in advance

115g (4oz) unsalted butter, gently melted
   and cooled, plus extra for the tin
450g (1lb) raspberries
juice of ½ lemon
225g (8oz) golden caster sugar,
   plus extra for the top
3 free-range eggs
250g (9oz) plain flour, sifted
2 rounded tsp baking powder
finely grated zest of 1 unwaxed lemon

1 Preheat the oven to 160°C/325°F/gas mark 3. Butter a 20cm (8in) round cake tin and line the base with greaseproof paper.

2 Place the raspberries and lemon juice in a mixing bowl. In another large bowl, whisk together the sugar and eggs until pale and thick, then carefully fold in the flour, baking powder and lemon zest. Stir in the butter.

3 Transfer the batter to the tin, then scatter in the raspberries and their juices. Sprinkle a little sugar over the top.

4 Bake for 1 hour, or until the cake springs back to the touch (*see* secret, below). Check the *torta* halfway through the cooking time – you may find you need to cover it with foil to prevent the top from scorching. Allow to cool in the tin, then turn out.

How to know when a cake is cooked
When a cake is cooked it will have an even colour, will be firm yet springy to the touch and should be slightly shrinking away from the edges of the tin. Insert a clean skewer right down into its centre. If it comes out clean, the cake is cooked. After removing it from the oven, give it a few minutes to rest in its tin before turning out on to a cooling rack.

Victoria sponge

A classic and a guilty pleasure, this is one of my favourite cakes. It's perfect with a cup of tea! I like raspberry jam as it's a little more tart than other jams, but do use strawberry jam if you like a sweeter filling.

Makes 8 slices
Preparation time 10 minutes,
   plus 2 hours cooling
Cooking time 20–25 minutes
Can be made in advance
Suitable for freezing

220g (8oz) unsalted butter, softened,
   plus extra for the tin
220g (8oz) caster sugar
3 large free-range eggs, lightly beaten
220g (8oz) self-raising flour
2 tbsp milk

For the butter icing
175g (6oz) icing sugar, sifted,
   plus 1 tsp extra to dust
85g (3oz) unsalted butter, softened
6 tbsp raspberry or strawberry jam

1 Preheat the oven to 180°C/350°F/gas mark 4. Butter two 20cm (8in) cake tins and line the bases with greaseproof paper.

2 Cream together the butter and caster sugar, using the paddle attachment of an electric mixer or by hand, (*see* secret, below). Add the eggs a little at a time, beating after each addition. Fold in the flour (*see* secret, page 254). Stir in the milk until the batter falls easily from a spoon.

3 Divide the batter evenly between the prepared cake tins and bake for 20–25 minutes, until the cakes are golden brown and a skewer inserted into the centre comes out clean. Remove from the oven and, as soon as you can handle the tins, turn out on to a wire rack and allow to cool completely.

4 To make the icing, beat the icing sugar and butter together in a large bowl until smooth and creamy. Spread a thick layer over the top of whichever cake looks less picturesque. Spread the jam over the base of the other half. Carefully sandwich together the cakes. Place 1 tsp icing sugar into a sieve and dust over the cake before serving.

How to cream a cake batter
Start with butter at room temperature, so you can work with it easily. If you have an electric mixer, creaming is easy, otherwise elbow grease works wonders! Beat the butter with the sugar for about 5 minutes, or until very light, pale and fluffy. Add the eggs a little at a time, beating well after each addition. If the mixture curdles, beat in 1 tbsp flour to bring it back together.

Cherry & almond loaf

This recipe belongs to my mother-in-law, Helen, and my son Jack thinks it is the best cake EVER... It is fantastic for a couple of days after baking as long as you keep it in an airtight container or wrap it in foil.

Makes 10 slices
Preparation time 10 minutes
Cooking time 50–55 minutes
Can be made in advance
Suitable for freezing

175g (6oz) unsalted butter, softened,
   plus extra for the tin
175g (6oz) caster sugar
finely grated zest of 1 unwaxed lemon
   and juice of ½ lemon
3 free-range eggs, beaten
225g (8oz) glacé cherries, rinsed and halved
75g (2¾oz) self-raising flour, sifted
75g (2¾oz) plain flour, sifted
pinch of salt
75g (2¾oz) ground almonds
splash of milk (optional)

1 Preheat the oven to 190°C/375°F/gas mark 5. Butter a 900g (2lb) loaf tin, then line it with greaseproof paper (*see* secret, below).

2 Cream together the butter, sugar, lemon zest and juice, using the paddle attachment of an electric mixer or by hand (*see* secret, page 246). Add the eggs a little at a time, beating after each addition.

3 Toss the cherries in a little of the flour to help them cling to the cake mixture instead of dropping to the bottom. Next, mix together the flours, salt, almonds and cherries and add to the batter, stirring well until the cherries are evenly distributed. The cake mixture needs to be fairly stiff, but add a splash of milk if you feel you need to.

4 Bake for 50–55 minutes, then test for doneness by inserting a skewer into the loaf's centre; if it comes out clean, it is done. If you find the top is browning too much before the loaf is ready, simply cover with foil and let it carry on baking.

5 Remove the loaf to a wire rack, leaving it in the greaseproof paper until cold.

Lining a cake tin
Using the tin as a template, cut out 2 strips of greaseproof paper. One should be the width of the tin's base and longer than the base and sides together, the other the length of the tin's base, again longer than the base and sides. Butter the tin and line it with the greaseproof paper, leaving overhanging pieces on each side to act as handles when the loaf is cooked.

Cupcake party time

Taking cake into school is the highlight of the year at my kids' school; to endear yourself to the teacher, make individual cakes to save them the stress of cutting even-sized pieces before 30 hawk-eyed children. That is, of course, if your helpful child remembers to tell you they're needed in time! For this recipe you'll need 20 cupcake cases.

Makes 20 cakes
Preparation time 20 minutes
Cooking time 15 minutes
Can be made in advance

175g (6oz) unsalted butter, softened
175g (6oz) caster sugar
2 large free-range eggs, beaten
1 tsp vanilla essence
175g (6oz) self-raising flour, sifted

For the icing
280g (10oz) icing sugar, sifted
2 drops red food colouring (optional)

For the decorations (optional)
mini marshmallows
white chocolate buttons
multicoloured sprinkles
hundreds and thousands
silver sprinkles

1 Preheat the oven to 180°C/350°F/gas mark 4.

2 Cream together the butter and caster sugar, using the paddle attachment of an electric mixer or by hand, until pale and fluffy (*see* secret, page 246). Add the eggs a little at a time, beating after each addition, then stir in the vanilla essence and fold in the flour (*see* secret, page 254).

3 Place the paper cases into a cupcake tray and fill each halfway full with the cake batter. Don't be tempted to overfill them as they will turn into a mess instead of a neatly contained cupcake.

4 Bake for 15 minutes, or until the cakes are golden and spring back to the touch.

5 Remove to a wire rack and leave until cold. (Do not try to ice the cakes until they are cold – it would be a disaster!)

6 To make the icing, place the icing sugar in a large bowl and beat in 3 tbsp water and the food colouring, if using (*see* secret, left).

7 Smooth the icing over the cakes with a palette knife, being generous. Sprinkle or arrange on any decorations that you or your child desire, while the icing is still wet. Put aside to allow the icing to set.

8 All that is left to do now is to place the cakes carefully on to a cake stand and avoid dropping them on the way into school!

The best glacé icing
Glacé icing should have a fairly stiff consistency after the water is added; if it doesn't, add more sugar until it does! If you use hot water you will get a shinier icing that's less likely to crack when it sets. It should be thick enough to leave a trail when trickled from a spoon back into the bowl. Replace some of the water with a squeeze of lemon or orange juice if you want a more flavoursome icing.

Chocolate heaven cupcakes

The pink Cupcake Party Time creations, with their sparkly sprinkles (see page 250), are far removed from anything my son would be seen taking into school. His idea of cakes is anything with chocolate, chocolate and more chocolate. For this recipe you'll need 18 cupcake cases.

Makes 18 cakes
Preparation time 20 minutes
Cooking time 15 minutes
Can be made in advance

175g (6oz) unsalted butter, softened
175g (6oz) caster sugar
2 large free-range eggs, beaten
175g (6oz) self-raising flour, sifted
25g (1oz) cocoa powder, sifted
white chocolate buttons, to decorate

For the butter icing
115g (4oz) unsalted butter, softened
175g (6oz) icing sugar, sifted
50g (1¾oz) cocoa powder, sifted

1 Preheat the oven to 180°C/350°F/gas mark 4.

2 Cream together the butter and caster sugar, using the paddle attachment of an electric mixer or by hand, until pale and fluffy (*see* secret, page 246). Add the eggs a little at a time, beating after each addition. Fold in the flour and cocoa powder (*see* secret, below).

3 Place the paper cases in a cupcake tray and fill each halfway full with the mixture. Don't be tempted to overfill them as they will turn into a mess instead of a neatly contained cupcake.

4 Bake for 15 minutes, or until the cakes are well risen and spring back to the touch. Remove to a wire rack and leave to cool completely.

5 To make the butter icing, place the butter, icing sugar and cocoa, along with 2 tbsp water, in a food processor with a whisk attachment, or into a large bowl (be prepared to use lots of elbow grease if you don't have the asset of electric beaters). Whisk for 5–10 minutes – the longer, the better – to give the icing lots of volume. It will become deliciously light and glossy.

6 Generously spread the icing on to the cupcakes with a palette knife. Decorate with white chocolate buttons, then serve.

How to fold in flour
After you have creamed together butter and sugar for a cake batter and added the eggs gradually, you need to retain the air thus created in the mixture to give the cakes their final lightness. To do so, sift the flour and fold it into the batter lightly, using a figure-of-eight motion and being careful not to beat out the air. Make sure that all traces of dry flour are well blended into the batter.

Garibaldi biscuits

Do you remember Garibaldis? My brothers called them squashed-fly biscuits and could never understand why I loved them so much. This is the closest I can get to a replica and is equally delicious. I have played around, adding lemon or orange zest, but the original version beats all.

Makes 20 biscuits
Preparation time 20 minutes
Cooking time 15–20 minutes
Can be made in advance

200g (7oz) plain flour
30g (1oz) cornflour
55g (2oz) caster sugar
pinch of salt
55g (2oz) butter, softened
1 free-range egg, separated
100ml (3½fl oz) milk
icing sugar, to dust
115g (4oz) currants

1 Preheat the oven to 190°C/375°F/gas mark 5.

2 Sift the flour and cornflour into a large bowl and stir in the sugar and salt. Add the butter, cut into knobs, and rub in with your fingertips until the mixture resembles breadcrumbs. Add the egg yolk and milk, and mix it all together to form a stiff dough.

3 Lightly dust a clean, dry work surface with icing sugar, dust your rolling pin too, and roll out the dough into a 30 × 20cm (12 × 8in) rectangle. Sprinkle the currants on to one half. Fold over the other half of the dough to cover the fruit and gently push together, sealing the edges by squashing them. Roll over the top with the rolling pin until the dough is about 5mm (¼in) thick, then cut into the traditional garibaldi rectangles, each about 6 × 3cm (2½ × 1¼in) in size. Prick each all over with a fork.

4 Line a baking sheet with greaseproof paper and spread out the biscuits over it. Brush the top of each with the egg white and bake for 15–20 minutes, or until golden brown. Remove from the oven and carefully transfer to a wire rack, using a palette knife, then set aside until cold. Sift over a little icing sugar to serve.

Storing cakes and biscuits

To keep biscuits, cookies and cakes fresh, seal them in an airtight container. An old biscuit tin is good for this. Always store them at room temperature, not in the refrigerator, to keep them tasting fresh and feeling crisp. Do not keep biscuits, cookies and cakes for more than a week, as they will be past their best.

Apple & raspberry crumble muffins

You will need a 12-hole muffin tin (which has deeper holes than a fairy-cake tin) and, ideally, some paper muffin cases. If you don't have muffin cases, see my secret, on page 260. The apple keeps these muffins very moist and this recipe is a handy way to use up those from the bottom of the fruit bowl that are past their best.

Makes 12 muffins
Preparation time 15 minutes
Cooking time 30–35 minutes
Can be made in advance

3 free-range eggs
180g (6oz) crème fraîche
250g (9oz) caster sugar
200g (7oz) plain flour, sifted
1½ tsp baking powder
1 apple, peeled, cored and finely chopped
150g (5½oz) raspberries

For the crumble topping
55g (2oz) unsalted butter, diced
55g (2oz) plain flour
25g (1oz) light muscovado sugar
1 tbsp roasted, chopped hazelnuts

1 Preheat the oven to 170°C/340°F/gas mark 3.

2 First make the crumble topping using the butter and flour (*see* secret, below). Stir in the muscovado sugar and hazelnuts. Set aside.

3 Place the eggs, crème fraîche, caster sugar, flour and baking powder into a bowl and mix together until smooth. Add the apple and half the raspberries and stir through, taking care not to crush the raspberries.

4 Place the paper cases into a muffin tin and half fill with the batter. Stir the remaining raspberries into the crumble topping and spoon this evenly on top.

5 Bake the muffins for 30–35 minutes, until golden and cooked through. When ready, they should spring back to the touch. Remove from the oven and allow to cool in the tin. These keep very well for a couple of days in an airtight container – the apple helps to keep the sponge really moist.

How to make a crumble topping

When making crumble topping, be sure you use cold butter. Add it to the flour and rub together very lightly with your fingertips, until the mixture resembles fine breadcrumbs and all the large lumps of butter have dispersed evenly. The warmth of your hands will soften the butter enough to blend with the flour. Stir in the remaining flavourings and the sugar. Don't overwork the topping, or it will be heavy and clumpy.

Carrot & raisin cupcakes

These cupcakes don't contain much fat but, of course, they contain vegetables, so they are relatively healthy...for cakes, at least! They provide the perfect energy boost between meals – just try not to eat too many! For this recipe, you will need a 12-hole cake tin and, ideally, some paper cake cases.

Makes 12 cakes
Preparation time 20 minutes
Cooking time 30 minutes
Can be made in advance

3 tbsp raisins
grated zest and juice of 1 unwaxed orange
4 free-range eggs, separated
225g (8oz) brown sugar
400g (14oz) ground walnuts
1 tsp ground cinnamon
350g (12oz) carrots, grated
175g (6oz) wholewheat flour
1 tsp baking powder

For the icing
225g (8oz) cream cheese
140g (5oz) icing sugar, sifted
grated zest and juice of 1 small
    unwaxed orange

1 Preheat the oven to 180°C/350°F/gas mark 4.

2 Place the raisins in a bowl with the orange zest and juice and leave to plump up for 10 minutes, or longer if you have the time.

3 Whisk together the egg yolks and brown sugar until thick and creamy. Add all the remaining ingredients except the egg whites and fold through until the mixture is nice and smooth. Beat the egg whites until they form stiff peaks when you remove the whisk, then carefully fold them into the cake mixture.

4 Place the paper cases into a cupcake tin and divide the batter between them. Bake the cupcakes in the oven for 30 minutes, until well risen and golden brown. Remove from the oven, place on a cooling rack and leave to cool completely.

5 Meanwhile, prepare the icing. Beat the cream cheese in a large bowl with the icing sugar until smooth. Add enough orange juice to reach your preferred consistency. Spread the icing over each cupcake and sprinkle with the orange zest.

Homemade cupcake cases
If you don't have any cake cases, cut suitably-sized discs of greaseproof paper or baking parchment and use them to line the cups in your cake tin instead.

Chocolate, fruit & nut cookies

Based on my favourite chocolate bar, fruit and nut, these cookies are a fantastic energy boost. Well, that's my excuse! Do ring the changes with this recipe; try replacing the milk chocolate with white, for instance, or using dried cranberries in place of the raisins.

Makes 35 cookies
Preparation time 10 minutes,
   plus 2 hours chilling
Cooking time 15–20 minutes
Can be made in advance

200g (7oz) unsalted butter, softened
250g (9oz) soft light brown sugar
2 free-range eggs, beaten
300g (10½oz) plain flour, sifted,
   plus extra to dust
1 tsp bicarbonate of soda
100g (3½oz) hazelnuts, lightly crushed
150g (5½oz) milk chocolate,
   in hazelnut-sized chunks
100g (3½oz) raisins

1 Cream together the butter and sugar, using the paddle attachment of an electric mixer or by hand, (*see* secret, page 246). Add the eggs a little at a time, beating after each addition, then fold in the flour and bicarbonate of soda. Stir in the hazelnuts, chocolate and raisins.

2 Flour a work surface and tip out the dough. Break it into 3 even-sized pieces and work each into a long sausage shape about 4–5cm (1½–2in) in diameter. Wrap tightly in clingfilm and refrigerate for a couple of hours (*see* secret, below).

3 When you are ready to bake the biscuits, preheat the oven to 180°C/350°F/gas mark 4. Line 2 baking sheets with greaseproof paper.

4 Remove the dough from the refrigerator and unwrap the clingfilm. Slice the dough sausages into 1cm (½in) wide slices and space them out well on the baking sheets – they will each spread about 1–2cm (½–¾in) all around. Bake the cookies for 15–20 minutes, or until golden brown. When they are done, transfer them immediately to a wire rack to stop the bottoms from burning.

Working with biscuit dough
Make sure the dough is not too wet or dry, or it will be difficult to shape into biscuits. As you practice, you will learn when to add more flour to a too-sticky dough, or milk to a dry mixture. Always refrigerate biscuit dough before baking; this helps to firm it up and stops the cookies spreading into one big flat mess in the oven.

Lemon & thyme shortbread

I have suggested thyme for these delicate biscuits, but you can always substitute lemon thyme if you are lucky enough to find it. Many supermarkets now stock it, so be sure to look out for it in the herb section. It will give the biscuits a more tangy flavour.

Makes about 48 biscuits
Preparation time 15 minutes,
  plus 2 hours chilling
Cooking time 10–15 minutes
Can be made in advance

400g (14oz) plain flour
2 tsp baking powder
pinch of salt
2 tbsp finely chopped thyme leaves
225g (8oz) unsalted butter, softened
300g (10½oz) golden caster sugar
2 tbsp finely grated unwaxed lemon zest
1 free-range egg, beaten
juice of 1 small lemon

1 Sift the flour and baking powder into a large bowl and stir in the salt and thyme.

2 Cream together the butter, sugar and lemon zest, using the paddle attachment of an electric mixer or by hand, until pale and fluffy (*see* secret, page 246). Add the egg a little at a time, beating after each addition, then slowly add the dry ingredients, stirring through well and dribbling in a little lemon juice until it comes together as dough. Do not add too much juice as the dough should not be too wet.

3 Roll the dough into 2 sausage shapes each about 5cm (2in) in diameter. This way, each will make a batch of 24 biscuits, so you could choose to save one batch for another time. Wrap each sausage tightly in clingfilm and refrigerate for at least 2 hours, or up to 2 days.

4 When you are ready to bake the shortbread, preheat the oven to 190°C/375°F/gas mark 5. Line a baking sheet with greaseproof paper.

5 Unwrap the clingfilm and slice the roll of dough into 5mm (¼in) thick biscuits. Spread these out on the baking sheet and bake for 10–15 minutes, until very slightly tinged with gold at the edges. Remove from the oven and carefully transfer to a wire rack, using a palette knife, then allow to cool completely.

Successful shortbread

I like flaky, light shortbread, not old-fashioned heavy slabs, so I cut the biscuits quite thin. It is important to refrigerate the dough until it feels really firm. If you chill it in the roll shape I suggest in this recipe and store in the refrigerator, you will also be ready simply to slice it into biscuits and impress guests with warm shortbread in just 15 minutes.

Gingerbread men & hearts

My children love these. Hearts and gingerbread men are my favourite cutter shapes and I find the sight of these biscuits enormously comforting. At Christmas time, try hanging a batch on the tree. Make sure they are eaten soon (that shouldn't be a problem!) or they will lose their crunch.

Makes 25 biscuits
Preparation time 10–15 minutes
Cooking time 12 minutes
Can be made in advance
Suitable for freezing at end of step 4

350g (12oz) plain flour, plus extra to dust
1 tsp ground ginger
½ tsp ground cloves
½ tsp ground cinnamon
1 tsp bicarbonate of soda
175g (6oz) soft brown sugar
100g (3½oz) unsalted butter, softened
1 free-range egg
4 tbsp golden syrup
splash of milk (optional)
175g (6oz) icing sugar, sifted
2 tbsp currants or raisins (optional)

Ground spices – the little and often rule

Spices are at their best when freshly ground and lose their fragrance and potency very quickly. To avoid dusty, tasteless spices, avoid buying them in large quantities. Instead, go for the smallest packets you can find and use them up soon after purchase. Any that you find hidden at the back of a shelf (and there will be the odd jar!) are best replaced with a fresh batch.

1 Preheat the oven to 180°C/350°F/gas mark 4.

2 Mix together the flour, spices, bicarbonate of soda and soft brown sugar in a large bowl, then add the butter, cut into knobs, and rub it in with your fingertips until the mixture resembles breadcrumbs.

3 Whisk together the egg and syrup and add to the dry ingredients, then knead until it forms a dough. You may need to add a very little milk, but the dough should not be wet or sticky.

4 Flour a work surface well and roll out the dough 5mm (¼in) thick. Choose some gingerbread men cutters – mine are about 7.5cm (3in) long – and some heart shapes and use to cut the dough.

5 Evenly space the gingerbread shapes on a baking sheet lined with greaseproof paper and bake for 12 minutes, or until golden brown. Remove from the oven, carefully transfer to a wire rack with a palette knife and allow to cool completely.

6 Mix the icing sugar with about 2 tbsp cold water to make a fairly thick icing that will coat the back of a spoon. Decorate the gingerbreads with the icing and add currant or raisin eyes, or buttons, to the man shapes if you like.

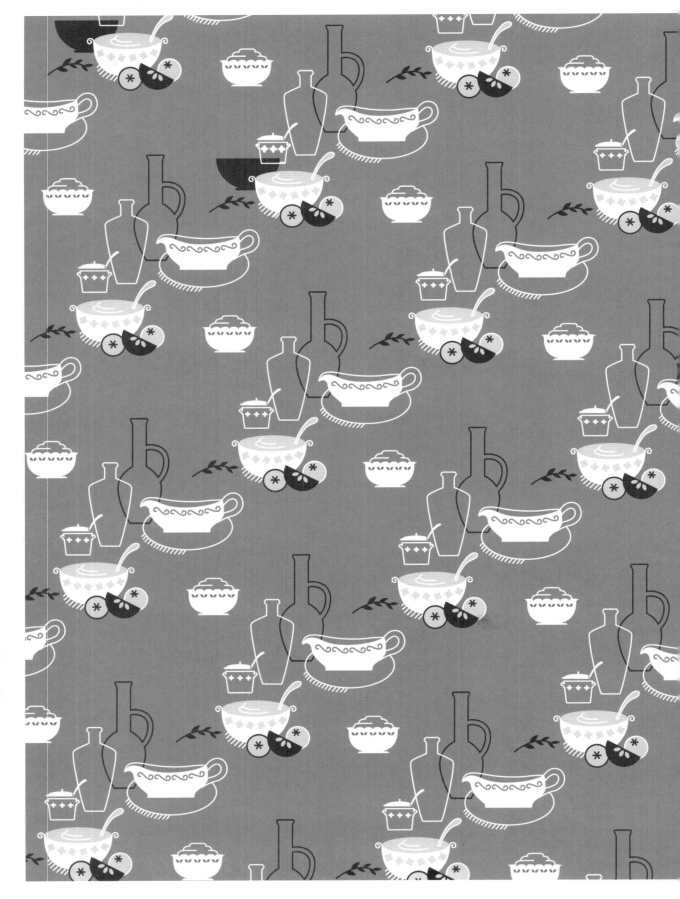

Sauces & dressings

Tomato & tarragon mayonnaise · Chilli & lime mayonnaise
Cheese dip · Creamy mustard vinaigrette
Homemade ranch-style dressing · Tomato sauce · Tomato salsa
Creamy corn salsa · Chunky apple sauce · Homemade gravy

Secrets of making sauces & dressings

Obviously, you can buy all your dressings, sauces and gravies in bottles at the supermarket. But I bet, if you read the labels, you'll be surprised by some of the ingredients. Do you really want to eat something if you can't understand what it is?

I strongly recommend you make your own mayonnaise. It's so satisfying and tastes wickedly delicious and indulgent. And it's not difficult to do. Just follow my instructions (*see* pages 272 and 274) and enjoy the process. Once you have tasted the incredible difference between this and shop-bought mayo, you'll never look back.

Homemade Ranch-style Dressing (*see* page 277) is a wonder condiment in our house. It's a great compromise between the simple vinaigrettes that I love and the creamier sauces that are Gordon's favourite. Use it for a chopped salad with chicken, beetroot and crumbled blue cheese, or have it with a plain green salad of Romaine lettuce.

Every Saturday night you'll find me glued to the television set watching 'X Factor' and eating crisps – my biggest weakness. The recipes for dips I give in this chapter are what I eat on the side. If you want to be more virtuous than me, have crudités or ciabatta toasts instead of crisps!

There's never an excuse for serving bought gravy. If you've gone to the trouble of selecting wonderful meat that has been farmed with care and properly butchered, my Homemade Gravy is what it deserves (*see* page 282). It's fairly hands off and not much effort to make – all you really need to remember is to keep scraping the pan.

Try to get into the habit of making Tomato Sauce (*see* page 278) in bulk, so you can store it. It's rich and deliciously easy, and you will feel so satisfied afterwards. The best thing is that most of the ingredients come from the storecupboard, so you will never be at a loss.

Tomato & tarragon mayonnaise

You really need a food processor or a stick blender to make this easily. There are big pieces of tomato here as it's quite a rustic recipe. If you want something more refined, simply cut the tomatoes more finely. This is great with cold chicken or when used to dress a potato salad.

Makes about 750ml (1¹⁄₃ pint)
Preparation time 10 minutes
Can be made in advance

150ml (5fl oz) olive oil
400ml (14fl oz) vegetable oil
3 free-range egg yolks
1 tbsp white wine vinegar
1 tsp English mustard
2 tsp chopped tarragon
180g (6½oz) cherry tomatoes, quartered
juice of ½ lemon
salt flakes and black pepper

1 Pour the oils into a large measuring jug.

2 Put the eggs, vinegar and mustard into a processor bowl and blend for 20 seconds, then slowly drizzle in the oils (*see* secret, below). As the mixture starts to thicken (you will hear the blade begin to make a different noise) pour the oil in a little faster.

3 When the mayonnaise is the right consistency, transfer it to a large bowl. Fold in the tarragon and tomatoes, followed by the lemon juice and seasoning. Keep in a sealed jar or covered bowl in the refrigerator for up to 2 days.

How to make mayonnaise

Don't be alarmed at the thought of making mayonnaise; it's really not difficult. The only trick is the speed at which you add the oil to room-temperature egg yolks. It needs to be poured in very slowly and patiently – literally drop by drop at first – while you whisk or process continuously to create an emulsion. You will see the sauce coming together. If it splits, start again with new egg yolks.

Chilli & lime mayonnaise

This is the perfect accompaniment to prawns, giving a new twist to a prawn cocktail. You can ring the changes on this recipe, omitting the chilli if serving it to children, or using lemon instead of lime. It will still be utterly moreish!

Serves 6–8
Preparation time 5 minutes
Can be made in advance

½ tsp chilli flakes
2 free-range egg yolks
juice of 1 lime
salt flakes and black pepper
310ml (10¼fl oz) vegetable oil

1 Put the chilli, egg yolks, lime juice and seasoning in the container that fits your hand blender, or into a food processor. Process together until frothy.

2 Gradually add the oil (*see* secret, page 272). The mayonnaise should be thick and glossy. If it is too thick, beat in a splash of water.

Cheese dip

My biggest weakness in life is crisps and dip in front of 'X Factor' on Saturday nights with the family. If you want a healthier option, try this dip alongside a platter of carrot and celery sticks, pieces of sweet pepper and crusty bread.

Serves 6–8
Preparation time 5 minutes
Can be made in advance

300g (10½oz) soft goats' cheese
100g (3½oz) cream cheese
4 tbsp double cream
3 tsp truffle oil (optional)
2 tbsp snipped chives
salt flakes and black pepper

1 Simply mix together the cheeses then add the cream and truffle oil (if liked). Finish by stirring through the chives and seasoning.

Don't be afraid of goats' cheese

I've lost count of how often I've heard friends say they don't like goats' cheese, and how many of the same people love this dip! These days, mild, creamy goats' cheese logs are as mellow as any other soft cheese and just as useful. I find that children love it and, of course, it's excellent for those with an intolerance to cows' milk. Keep the strong, whiffy, hard goats' cheese for aficionados.

Creamy mustard vinaigrette

This is the perfect dressing for a chunky dish such as mixed bean salad, as the creaminess coats the beans. It's versatile and great poured over almost any salad, so it's good to have a jar in the refrigerator to be used at any time.

Makes about 180ml (5½fl oz)
Preparation time 5 minutes
Can be made in advance

6 tbsp olive oil
2 tbsp white wine vinegar
2 tbsp grain mustard
2 tbsp crème fraîche
salt flakes and black pepper

1 Place all the dressing ingredients into a jug – or transfer them to a clean jam jar with a lid – and whisk briskly (or shake the jar) until the vinaigrette has a smooth, creamy appearance. Taste and adjust the seasoning, making sure the balance of flavours is as you like it; you can add more of any ingredient to suit your palate. Store in the refrigerator until required.

2 Always leave it until the last moment before dressing a salad, and give the vinaigrette a final whisk or shake before pouring.

How to make the perfect vinaigrette

Vinaigrette combines oil and vinegar to give a smooth, emulsified dressing. In this recipe I have used grain mustard as this helps the emulsion to hold. The crème fraîche gives a creamy finish. Always remember to season a dressing as this will bring out the taste. Store in the refrigerator until needed, although I would use it within 2 days.

Homemade ranch-style dressing

Use different herbs from those suggested below to suit your taste, or spring onions for a bit of crunch. This dressing works well for salads, as a dipping sauce, or with jacket potatoes. As a family, we all have different favourite salad dressings, but this manages to appeal to all of us.

Serves 6–8
Preparation time 5 minutes
Can be made in advance

125ml (4fl oz) mayonnaise
125ml (4fl oz) sour cream
125ml (4fl oz) buttermilk
1 tbsp snipped chives
1 tsp finely chopped parsley leaves
1 tsp finely chopped dill fronds
1 garlic clove, crushed
salt flakes and black pepper

1 Simply mix all the ingredients together really well, season to taste and serve at room temperature.

Buttermilk: the secret weapon
It's always worth having a pot of tangy, yogurty buttermilk in the refrigerator as it has so many uses. You will find it in most larger supermarkets. As well as giving a flavour boost to my dressing recipe here, it can act as a raising agent in yeast-free baking, such as for Irish soda bread or scones. Its slight acidity also makes it a valuable ingredient in marinades for chicken, where it acts as a tenderiser.

Tomato sauce

This is great for pasta sauces or pizza toppings. Make a large batch and cook it slowly until it begins to thicken and its flavours intensify, filling the house with a lovely aroma. This is a base sauce, so it's very adaptable; try adding pancetta, marinated peppers or mushrooms.

Makes 1.1kg (2½lb)
Preparation time 10 minutes
Cooking time 30 minutes
Can be made in advance
Suitable for freezing

drizzle of olive oil
2 red onions, finely sliced
2 garlic cloves, finely sliced
200ml (7fl oz) red wine
3 × 400g cans peeled cherry tomatoes
generous dash of Worcestershire sauce
handful of basil leaves, roughly sliced
salt flakes and black pepper

1 Pour the olive oil into a large pan and place over a medium heat. When it's hot, add the onions and garlic and gently fry for 3–4 minutes, until softened. Add the red wine and allow to reduce for a few minutes until the liquid has almost evaporated.

2 Add the tomatoes and heat through, then add the Worcestershire sauce and basil and bring to a simmer. Bubble gently for 20–25 minutes, or until the sauce starts to thicken.

3 Season to taste, then allow to cool completely before refrigerating.

Tomato salsa

Again, I have this on my crisps! But this is a far more versatile recipe and is fabulous with cold chicken, alongside any salad or used as a topping over a crunchy bruschetta (see page 200). All in all, a very useful thing to have stashed away in the refrigerator.

Serves 6–8
Preparation time 10 minutes
Can be made in advance

335g (11¾oz) baby vine tomatoes, quartered
3 tbsp olive oil
1 red chilli, deseeded and finely chopped
1 small red onion, finely chopped
3 spring onions, finely chopped
2 tbsp balsamic vinegar
1 tsp sesame oil
1 tbsp finely chopped coriander or basil
salt flakes

1 Mix together all the ingredients and season to taste. Chill in the refrigerator until ready to serve.

How to choose the best tomatoes
Always keep a look out for the reddest, most plump and aromatic fruits you can find. The ripest tomatoes are often revealed by their lovely herbal scent. Go for tomatoes that are blemish- and bruise-free and have a little 'give' when lightly pressed.

Creamy corn salsa

This makes a nice accompaniment to cold meats, especially ham and salami, and cheese and potatoes, either hot or cold. It's always an indispensable part of a bits-and-pieces family lunch, with lots of salads on the table, for us all to help ourselves.

Serves 6–8
Preparation time 5 minutes
Can be made in advance

325g can sweetcorn, drained
1 red chilli, deseeded and finely chopped
2 ripe plum tomatoes, cut into
   1cm (½in) dice
1 garlic clove, finely chopped
juice of ½ lime
1 tbsp maple syrup
2 tbsp sour cream
salt flakes and black pepper
1 tbsp finely chopped coriander leaves

1 Mix together all the ingredients and allow the flavours to fuse in the refrigerator until ready to use.

The best fresh sweetcorn

For this dish, I have used canned sweetcorn. However, if you choose fresh corn, make sure you select plump-looking cobs, with bright green, stiff husks and no sign of dry or shrivelled kernels. Remove the husks, pull away all the 'silk' (the hairs you will find inside) and carefully cut down the cob lengthways to remove the kernels, using a sharp knife. Rinse. Use the kernels as soon as possible, so they retain the maximum sweetness. Cook them in a pan of water for 2–3 minutes, or until tender, then drain. If you are not using all the kernels, you can easily freeze them for use later.

Chunky apple sauce

I use Braeburn apples to give a textured sauce as they don't break down into a mush. They have a lovely sweet yet tangy taste that is a wonderful accompaniment to my Crackling Roast Pork (see page 27). If you prefer a smoother sauce, try Granny Smith or Bramley apples instead.

Serves 6
Preparation time 10 minutes
Cooking time 20–25 minutes
Can be made in advance

6 Braeburn apples
small knob of butter
squeeze of lemon juice
1 tbsp sugar
splash of water

1 Peel and core the apples and cut into 1cm (½in) cubes. Place them in a pan with the butter, then cook immediately over a medium heat (*see* secret, below).

2 Cook the apples for 20–25 minutes, stirring frequently, until softened. Add the lemon juice and sugar and a splash or two of cold water, until you have the consistency you like.

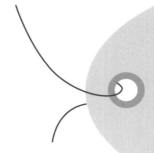

Preventing discolouration

It is important to begin to cook apples as soon as they are prepared, or they will begin to oxidise and turn an unpleasant brown colour. To keep apples beautifully white in a fruit salad, toss them through lemon juice immediately after cutting. This will protect the slices from discolouration. The same applies to avocado in guacamole recipes (try lime to preserve the colour), or the cut edges of fresh artichokes.

Homemade gravy

The most important thing to remember for excellent gravy is to let the meat catch very slightly on the base of the roasting tin, so you can scrape up all the sticky, deeply savoury bits into the sauce. Don't let it burn, though, or it will be too bitter to serve.

Makes about 700–750ml
   (1¼–1⅓ pints)
Preparation time 10 minutes
Cooking time 1 hour 15 minutes
Can be made in advance
Suitable for freezing

1kg (2lb 4oz) chicken wings
1 tbsp tomato purée
6 garlic cloves, skin on, crushed
1 onion, roughly chopped
3 thyme sprigs
100ml (3½fl oz) white wine
1.2 litres (2 pints) chicken stock
   (*see* page 37)
salt flakes and black pepper

1 Preheat the oven to 190°C/375°F/gas mark 5.

2 Place the chicken wings in a flameproof roasting dish or a deep, heavy roasting tin and cook for 45–50 minutes, or until golden brown. Remove the chicken from the dish then transfer the dish to the hob over a medium heat.

3 Stir the tomato purée, garlic and onion into the chicken juices in the dish, scraping the chicken bits off the bottom. Add the thyme, wine and stock. Increase the heat and bring to the boil, continuing to scrape all the lovely browned bits from the base of the dish (this is where the flavour is). Let the gravy reduce for 15–20 minutes.

4 Give the gravy a final scrape, then pass it through a sieve. Taste and season. If you would like a thicker consistency, boil down a little further.

Gravy tricks
Any piece of meat large enough to roast will give plenty of excellent gravy, especially if cooked on a bed of root vegetables. Add red wine or water to beef juices; red or white wine or stock to lamb; wine, cider or apple juice to pork; white wine to chicken. Always scrape in the bits from the base of the tin, then reduce the liquid by half. For thicker gravy you may need to stir in flour before the liquid.

Index

To Gordon, Megan, Jack, Holly and Matilda, the best team x

THANKS

I would like to thank so many people for so much help, support and fun with this book.

Karen Taylor, so incredibly organised, efficient and calm throughout – having three sons, she is not phased by anything! Thanks also to Chris Taylor, for all his help and hard work, along with stories of his rock band to entertain... Lisa Harrison for helping with recipe testing – having your eagle eye over my recipes is very comforting! Paula, Pene and Sarah, the shoots all ran so smoothly and everything looks so beautiful with all your creative inputs, thank you. Laura, I love all your photos, the recipes look amazing, the colours vibrant and fun.

Thanks also to Lucy Bannell – I have a huge amount of admiration for you working and turning things around at the speed you do with baby twins; you make it look effortless! I am still trying to figure it out and my twins are ten!

Thanks to Leanne Bryan, for ensuring the detail is just right, and to Becca Spry for putting together such a lovely team for me to work with and making it such an enjoyable project; I have loved every minute and having you there for ideas and banter has been brilliant.

Lastly, thanks to Martine Carter, for bringing it all together.

Tana Ramsay

Tana's Kitchen Secrets
by Tana Ramsay

First published in Great Britain in 2010 by Mitchell Beazley, an imprint of Octopus Publishing Group Limited, Endeavour House, 189 Shaftesbury Avenue, London, WC2H 8JG
www.octopusbooks.co.uk

An Hachette UK Company
www.hachette.co.uk

Copyright © Octopus Publishing Group Ltd 2010
Text copyright © Tana Ramsay 2010
Photography copyright © Laura Hynd 2010

All rights reserved. No part of this work may be reproduced or utilised in any form or by any means, electronic or mechanical, including photocopying, recording, or by any information storage and retrieval system, without the prior written permission of the publishers.

The publishers will be grateful for any information that will assist them in keeping future editions up to date. Although all reasonable care has been taken in the preparation of this book, neither the publishers nor the author can accept any liability for any consequence arising from the use thereof, or the information contained therein.

The author has asserted her moral rights.

ISBN: 978 1 84533 511 3

A CIP record for this book is available from the British Library.

Set in Berling LT and Justlefthand

Printed and bound in China

Commissioning Editor Becca Spry
Senior Editor Leanne Bryan
Art Director Pene Parker
Senior Art Editor Juliette Norsworthy
Designer Paula Macfarlane
Copy-editor Lucy Bannell
Photographer Laura Hynd
Home Economists Lisa Harrison, Karen Taylor, Robert Allison and Chris Taylor
Stylist Sarah O'Keefe
Proofreader Ruth Baldwin
Indexer Hilary Bird
Production Manager Peter Hunt

With thanks to:

Summerill & Bishop
100 Portland Road,
London, W11 4LQ
tel: 020 7727 1322
www.summerillandbishop.com

Ceramica Blue
10 Blenheim Crescent,
London, W11 1NN
tel: 020 7727 0288
email: shop@ceramicablue.co.uk
www.ceramicablue.co.uk